W9-DJE-981

**Learning
To Apply
New Concepts
to Casework Practice**

LEARNING
TO APPLY
NEW CONCEPTS
TO CASEWORK PRACTICE

Gertrude Einstein, editor

A STAFF DEVELOPMENT SEMINAR

Family Service Association of America
44 East 23rd Street, New York, N.Y. 10010

FOREWORD

The voluntary family service agency will merit community support as long as its operations include the elements of innovation and flexibility. These elements are indispensable to the search for new answers to old questions and new methods with which to treat, or deal with, the increasingly complex personal and family problems brought to the agency each day. The new methods required can be evolved only as social workers gain more knowledge. The agency's responsibility for advancing knowledge is discharged in great part through its staff development program, the primary goal of which is to improve the quality and effectiveness of the agency's services. We have learned that high standards of service cannot be maintained unless the agency has a thoughtfully planned, continuous process of staff education.

The staff development seminar has long been an important medium of staff training. It is a vital supplement to the program of regular staff supervision. In most settings, responsibility for the planning of staff seminars—subject matter, leadership, participants, and timing—is assumed collaboratively by the administrative staff and the supervisory staff.

The Jewish Family Service of Philadelphia is indebted to its director of professional services, Gertrude Einstein, for her leadership, teaching skill, and inspiring and contagious spirit of adventure in the pursuit of learning and knowledge. These qualities helped make the seminar reported in this volume an outstanding learning experience for all who participated. The agency is also indebted to the lecturers for their excellent, apt, and stimulating theoretical contributions to the seminar.

Although the seminar was held during 1964 and 1965, we have been persuaded by the Family Service Association of America to permit the publication of the proceedings at this time. It is our hope that family service agencies, public welfare departments, and other organizations engaged in casework practice will find the report useful in structuring their own staff development programs.

Appreciation is extended to Miss Einstein for editing the proceedings and to the Family Service Association of America for its interest and support.

BENJAMIN R. SPRAFKIN
EXECUTIVE DIRECTOR
JEWISH FAMILY SERVICE OF PHILADELPHIA
PHILADELPHIA, PENNSYLVANIA

June 1968

Contributors

GERTRUDE EINSTEIN, *Director of Professional Services, Jewish Family Service of Philadelphia, Philadelphia, Pennsylvania.*

ROBERT L. LEOPOLD, M.D., *Associate Professor of Clinical Psychiatry, and Director, Division of Community Psychiatry, University of Pennsylvania, Philadelphia, Pennsylvania; Director, West Philadelphia Community Mental Health Consortium, Philadelphia, Pennsylvania.*

OTTO POLLAK, PH.D., *Professor of Sociology, University of Pennsylvania, Philadelphia, Pennsylvania.*

JOHN P. SPIEGEL, M.D., *Professor of Social Psychiatry, Florence Heller Graduate School for Advanced Studies in Social Welfare, Brandeis University, Waltham, Massachusetts.*

CONTENTS

INTRODUCTION:
PLANNING AND CARRYING OUT
A STAFF DEVELOPMENT SEMINAR

Gertrude Einstein

In-service staff training has been accepted by most casework agencies as an indispensable element of their programs.

There is no doubt that the recent graduate with a master's degree in social work needs additional training. He has gained both broad and basic knowledge through his classroom and field work and developed the attitudes and beginning skills needed in offering casework service. But he must have help in learning additional concepts and skills, as they apply to the specific functions he will have to perform as a beginning worker. In the family agency, for example, the novice and the worker with limited experience have much to learn about family dynamics, about the agency's specific functions, and about the differential use of a variety of interviewing methods—individual, joint, family, and group.

The experienced worker, on the other hand, presumably has a firm grasp of the agency's functions, but he needs the opportunity to keep up-to-date with new developments and changes in the field. Though he reads the books in the agency's library and attends conferences as often as he can, he finds keeping up-to-date outside an academic setting a major challenge.

The goal of an in-service training program is necessarily service-related. Neither for the recent graduate nor for the experienced practitioner can training focus on professional growth and development as it does for the full-time student. The voluntary casework agency has a mandate from the community; it has been established to help clients solve certain defined problems; it is accountable, qualitatively and quantitatively, to a board of directors and, through the board, to the community it serves. Consequently,

1

the amount of staff time set aside for training must be reasonably related to the amount of time devoted to direct service to clients and to the many ancillary activities the agency must engage in if it is to be an integral part of the community. Moreover, an in-service training program must be closely enough related to the agency's services to hold promise that, through it, the agency's program will be improved and its services made more effective.

In-service training programs must be planned with three main factors in mind: (1) the needs of the agency; (2) the needs of the professional staff; and (3) the new concepts and methods emerging in social work practice. Each of these factors will be touched on briefly.

Before setting up a staff training program, the agency administrator should analyze the agency program as a whole. How well-balanced is the composite of the services offered? Are the services truly available in that they are known to the community? In what parts of the program are there lacks or weaknesses? For example, have the community's senior citizens brought their problems to the agency, and have they been served? Has the agency served hard-to-reach, multiproblem families? Have parents requested help for their younger children as well as for their adolescents? If any of these groups has not used programed service, despite the agency's intent to serve them, is it because the staff lacks certain skills? Does the agency use a variety of helping methods? Does its staff utilize individual, joint, family, and group counseling methods differentially? If not, could new knowledge help fill the gap? Has the agency failed to teach staff members what they need to know, or has in-service training not "taken"?

An analysis based on questions of this kind can lead the administrator to institute special training in one or more areas of knowledge for the whole staff or for selected staff members. And such in-service training can enable the agency to establish special services for various categories of clients and to adopt new methods of service. The level of experience and skill of the staff as a whole is an important consideration for determining the nature of a training program. The supervisory staff should be asked what additional knowledge workers need in order to perform at the level expected by the agency—which, itself, must be defined. In recent years it has been stressed that the field of social work has no more a right than any other profession to ask its workers to "grow" unendingly, but, at the same time, some workers are eager for further learning and want help in applying new concepts in the interest of giving more effective service.

To devise an appropriate in-service training program one must know certain characteristics of the staff. How much training and experience does each staff member have? On what level does he function? In what areas are his strengths and weaknesses? His special interests? What has been offered to staff members through supervision or in past staff seminars and staff meetings? What learning needs have been brought to the supervisors' attention by the staff members themselves? And finally, what is the common denominator of a wide variety of staff needs and interests?

In planning a staff development program one must also take into account new theory and experimental practice. What new ideas in casework, group work, psychiatry, or sociology may have pertinence to agency program and

2

practice? Should some concepts in the agency's basic theoretical framework be changed or abandoned in favor of new ones? Which of the new ideas fit into agency philosophy, function, and structure? Are there effective new methods of which staff members are not aware? If they are aware of these new methods, is there a gap between their knowledge and their practice? Teaching material must be selected carefully; it should be in keeping with the identity of the agency but not rigidly patterned only to the known and tried.

In sum, to be effective, a staff training program must be the outcome of careful administrative planning, must be an integral part of the administrative process, and must be related to agency program and goals and to changing community needs.

It was with these guidelines in mind that the Jewish Family Service of Philadelphia designed and carried out the in-service training seminar reported in this volume, through which, it is hoped, their applicability and application will be spelled out in a way that may be helpful to others.

The starting point for the planning was, of course, the nature and identity of the agency itself. It is a sectarian family agency, serving a community of 300,000. It serves about 1,000 families a month. It has three district offices, and its professional staff of about thirty includes an executive director, a director of professional services, and four case supervisors. All the supervisors carry caseloads. Some of the caseworkers are employed part time. A large proportion of the workers can be classified as "very experienced," having been professionally employed for periods of from ten to twenty years. During each academic year, the agency trains from six to eight first-year, second-year, or doctoral students.

Each year, in the spring, the executive director, the director of professional services, and the four case supervisors discuss the staff's training needs in preparation for the training program to be begun in the fall. From among the numerous topics suggested, two general ones were selected for concentration for the seminar to be reported in this volume: the intake of applicants in crisis and family group treatment.

Intake methods are always crucial, for if the client is not helped to move into a relationship with the agency and cannot be held long enough to begin working on his problem, the most ingeniously devised casework services will prove to be of no avail. All family agencies lose a number of clients immediately after application, or after the first interview in the agency, despite the client's apparent need for continuing service. And so the question was raised during one of the seminar planning meetings whether the staff was always sufficiently attuned to recognizing crisis situations and moving effectively and rapidly in offering help. While we were fully aware that many clients were coming to us at a point of more or less acute crisis, it seemed to us that some observations and thoughts, organized as a "theory of crisis," could help us hold some of the clients we were losing and define more accurately the appropriate level of intervention. Since all staff members are involved in intake in our agency, this topic seemed to be of primary importance.

Under the leadership of our psychiatric consultant we had invested much

3

time, effort, and money in our family group treatment program. We had installed a one-way screen and speaker and a tape recorder. The agency's most experienced personnel had done the pioneering work. We were at a point at which we wished to involve more staff members in conducting family interviews, not occasionally, but systematically and consistently.

Three kinds of theory that had been useful to us in coming to an understanding of the family as a gestalt were role theory, family structure and function, and basic values. The fields of anthropology, sociology, and psychology had provided us with a considerable amount of literature in these areas, some of which had direct implications for family counseling. We wished to explore further the applicability of relevant theoretical constructs in work with troubled families.

Because of the degree of sophistication and length of experience of the majority of our staff members, we decided to try a new format for the seminar. First, creative leaders in their respective fields would be invited to address the staff, to provide a stimulating and exciting point of departure for our subsequent staff sessions. Clearly, however, stimulation is not a goal in itself. We wanted to be reasonably certain, in addition, that some of the new ideas would be absorbed and, ultimately, transformed into practice skills. Consequently, we planned, after each lecture, two group discussion sessions, to be led by the director of professional services. In the first session the main ideas that had been presented were to be identified, summarized, and analyzed. In the second session illustrative material from the workers' own cases was to be presented and discussed in the light of the theoretical concepts under consideration. Since it is an accepted fact that regardless of a worker's level of knowledge and experience he is likely to have some resistance to learning, we thought it important that the theoretical and practice sessions be held in sequence, so that the staff could achieve some balance between receptivity and active participation. The entire professional staff (with the exception of first-year students) was invited to attend the seminar, but attendance was voluntary. All staff members, full time and part time, including second-year students, decided to attend and continued to do so throughout.

The lecturers we secured are authorities in their respective fields and, at the same time, experienced teachers. They are interested in community psychiatry and public health questions or have done research in the family, its structure, its functions, and its value orientations. All of them have some knowledge of family service agencies and have had enough contact with trained social workers to accept and respect them as professional colleagues.

At the first seminar session the director of professional services announced the seminar topics, the names of the lecturers, and the particular expertise each could bring to the topics chosen. She then reviewed the agency's past experience in family group treatment, which had included consultation by experts, the delineation of a methodological approach to family group treatment under the leadership of the agency's psychiatric consultant, and an analysis by the case supervisors of the first cases carried in family group treatment. Three senior workers who had attended a seminar on family group treatment at the Philadelphia Psychiatric Center and all the workers who had conducted family interviews were invited to tell the group about their experiences.

All staff members displayed a keen interest in both crisis theory and family group treatment, evidenced by their many questions, their responsiveness to the experiences described by those who had been actively engaged in family interviewing, and their eagerness to take on the role of learner. Before the session adjourned, a reading list was distributed.

In the final session, after discussing the application to several cases of the concepts presented in the seminar, we evaluated the total seminar experience in terms of content and format. Some of the comments that were made stressed the stimulating nature of the ideas set forth by the guest lecturers. One counselor commented on the particular utility of the concept of subculture and of making reference to specific cultural value systems; she now found herself moving more slowly and looking more closely at cultural factors before developing a diagnosis and setting treatment goals for a particular family. Although participants had felt under some pressure to prepare illustrative case material, they were unanimous in their judgment that the seminar format was an excellent medium for learning. The sessions devoted to case presentations and staff discussions had served as a connecting link between the highly theoretical concepts of the guest lecturers and their own day-to-day practice.

The director of professional services, who had served as discussion leader for all the sessions and had periodically summarized the main points made, offered a final challenge to the groups: Which of the concepts discussed were most directly relevant for casework practice? Had the seminar taught us to ask new questions and seek new answers that might increase our helpfulness to clients?

The following questions were formulated:

Crisis Intervention

1. In coming to the agency for help, does the applicant experience his situation as a crisis?

2. How anxious is he? How fearful? How ready for help?

3. How has he dealt with stress in the past? What are his tools for coping? What kind of support system does he have? How strong is it?

4. On what level should the counselor intervene—the environmental level, the level of interpersonal relationships, or both? What should the goals be?

5. How fast or slowly should the counselor move?

Role Theory

1. How do the family members define their roles? How do their values affect their role definitions?

2. What are the mutual role expectations of family members—parent and child, husband and wife, sibling and sibling? Have these expectations been made explicit?

3. How does the counselor define family roles? What modification does he see as necessary? What forces seem to keep roles fixed? Are there role discrepancies?

5

Family Structure and Function

1. How well do the members of a client family fulfill their family functions? Where have they failed, and where have they succeeded? Does the applicant see any connection between the failure in functioning and the problem that caused him to seek help?

2. What qualities make a man a man and a woman a woman? How does the answer to this question affect the counseling process in general? How does it affect the counseling process with a specific couple?

Cultural Values

1. What values does the family hold? Are its goals related to these values? Are they goals held in common, or are there discrepancies between the goals of various members? Which values does the counselor support, and which ones does he question?

2. Does a particular family have characteristics related specifically to its Jewish heritage? Do its values differ from those generally held in our society?

The Family Approach in Counseling

1. What is the family gestalt? How does *this* family function? How do its members communicate or fail to communicate? Are there any alliances? Which are the areas of trouble? Which are the areas of strength? How does the family interact with the kinship system? How does it interact with the community?

2. How do the various family members affect each other? How well is the change through counseling of one family member tolerated by the others? Is the change being resisted and, therefore, "undone"?

3. How are decisions made? Who is the leader?

4. How does understanding the family as a whole affect counseling goals for each member? How is it reflected in the structuring and timing of interviews?

No attempt was made to answer these questions; they were set forth as stimuli to further thought. It was acknowledged that new ideas are not easily absorbed, and that some resistance is inherent in all learning. It was the responsibility of the supervisors, therefore, to keep the new concepts alive, to help make them a part of the agency's general theoretical base, and to stimulate the counselors to continue to test them in practice.

Social casework in general—and family counseling in particular—requires knowledge and skill, basic theory, and imagination. The seminar was designed to provide intellectual stimulation and to encourage a critical, individualized, imaginative use of new concepts in day-to-day work with clients. It is always difficult to gauge the impact of a learning experience. But staff members had found the seminar sufficiently valuable and enjoyable to request similar opportunities in the future.

This volume presents, in condensed form, the proceedings of the seminar sessions. Editorial judgment has been exercised in deleting irrelevant matter and highlighting that part of the seminar content deemed to have the greatest interest to social workers engaged in casework practice in other settings.

CRISIS INTERVENTION:
SOME NOTES ON PRACTICE AND THEORY

Robert L. Leopold

In the field in which psychiatry and social work operate jointly, crisis theory represents one of those areas that have been explicated in fairly formal terms only within the past decade. Yet one can see the beginnings of what is now called crisis theory as long ago as the 1940's in some of the work of Erich Lindemann, for example, his work following the Cocoanut Grove fire in Boston.[1] In a sense, crisis theory appears to constitute a historic turnabout. It seems to shift the focus of our attention from the individual to the environment; it seems to reverse the feeling, held for so long by so many workers in the field of individual therapy, that the individual psyche and its intrapsychic aspects are all-important and that the social structure has little or no part in the therapist's problems. But we in the field know intuitively that there has been no such sudden shift. The field operated with due regard for the social aspects of individual problems for fifty years prior to formal explication of crisis theory. But it was not quite respectable to admit it. Now, however, it *is* acceptable to talk about crisis, to discuss human beings in terms of their here-and-now functioning, and to look within them intrapsychically only when the psyche becomes a relevant field of investigation.

---

[1] Stanley Cobb and Erich Lindemann, "Neuropsychiatric Observations" (from Symposium on The Management of the Cocoanut Grove Burns at the Massachusetts General Hospital), *Annals of Surgery*, Vol. CXVII, June 1943, pp. 814–24, and Erich Lindemann, "Symptomatology and Management of Acute Grief," *The American Journal of Psychiatry*, Vol. CI, September 1944, pp. 141–48.

PATTERNS OF RESPONSE

Because intervention in crisis is a common-sense kind of thing that we all do, it seems very ordinary and the problems attendant on it appear almost too simple to talk about. The process appears to be plain enough: the caretaker receives a call for help, and he responds in any appropriate professional way. This, of course, is a very broad statement that covers a great many ways of approaching a situation. Caretaking in a small, tightly knit community does permit a kind of response that is relatively intuitive and empathic. There is no need there for the development of techniques that are specific to the urban community. This is true also in the somewhat larger community in which there is a one-purpose agency or office. Everything that comes along there is your problem; you respond to requests for help because you have no choice. At the other end of the pole is the complex society in which there begins to take place what Ralph Kaufmann so intriguingly termed "the game of musical agencies." This term is appropriate to a society characterized by specialization, professionalization, and the rise of institutions as substitutes for human beings in taking care of people. In such a society, we become involved in a host of bureaucratic considerations that often tend to take the spontaneous human element out of caretaking. I think that crisis theory, in a sense, developed in response to a need to put the human being back in the middle of the crisis where he belongs, instead of letting him be an input for a social or medical machine, a statistic that waits in line in a computer and is dealt with subsequently when an agency has time for it.

In other words, I believe that our pattern of response in a complex urban society is neither a simple human one nor one that fits an ideal professional model—one that all of us could draw. If we asked a roomful of people how a professional caretaker should respond ideally to a person in crisis, I suspect we should get a reasonable consensus about what should be done. But, then, if we went around again asking each individual whether he had the time, and the wish, to get into all the heartache and dirtying of hands involved in doing what had been agreed upon, I believe we should get some backing-down—not because any of us wishes to depart from the ideal professional model, but because there is so little time available in the face of enormous demands.

It seems to me that our pattern of response, in reality rather than according to the ideal, is conditioned by a composite of circumstances: by professional training, by exigency, by conflicting demands, by institutional procedures, and even by such minutiae as telephone calls about which we are annoyed, because secretaries do not put them through or because they do. Since a composite of circumstances—either these or others that are likewise only more or less subject to control—is likely always to condition the response pattern, it appears that there is a need for us to re-evaluate realistically our ways of responding as human beings who are concerned with the care of other human beings. This is true whether we are psychoanalysts, caseworkers, recreation workers, or supporting personnel in any way connected with the caretaking situation.

Here I want to digress for a moment to add a cautionary word about reality. Reality is a strange phenomenon. For example, "But I already have a full caseload" or "This is not a proper place for me" may indeed be realistic responses. But one may use the reality as a way of rationalizing one's unconscious needs. These statements may actually mean, "This is something I don't feel very comfortable about doing." All of us tend to let our blind spots limit our view of what we can do or should attempt to do. This is why we have supervisors and why supervisors themselves need supervisors. In effect, this is why, in any first-rate setup, people supervise each other, no matter what their hierarchical rank. In my own special field of interest, social psychiatry, there is little formal supervision, because the field is developing without much hierarchical procedure. The small group of psychiatrists now working in the field have to create their own informal supervision. We supervise each other in good, but too infrequent, sessions; we learn by talking about our problems and getting assistance with them from the thinking of others.

We psychiatrists have another problem affecting our patterns of response, which is familiar to all social workers. This problem relates to categories. Often the category into which we place a person or family at the beginning of a case determines, in itself, the kind of service we render indefinitely thereafter. In some ways this categorization is necessary. An agency with a large caseload cannot be run effectively unless cases are categorized in some measure. The research people tell us that doing so is absolutely essential, and the epidemiologists spend much time arguing that we should.

Granting the necessity for categorizing in some areas, it is clear that we are frequently deprived of the immediate human response by putting a label on a situation and then treating it as if the label told the absolute truth about it. For example, I was recently called on to attend a young girl who was representative of a type frequently encountered in both psychiatric and social work practice, an acutely psychotic eighteen-year-old. She had had an automobile accident in which her hip had been badly broken. She had been admitted to a hospital and, while there, had had an acute psychotic episode. The physician attending her had told her family she was schizophrenic and should be transferred to another hospital for electroshock treatment. Thus she was categorized, and a decision for action was made on the basis of the categorization. Then the family called me. I said I did not like the diagnosis of schizophrenia for young people only eighteen years of age, particularly after only three days of observation. The girl was brought to a hospital in my locality. She was indeed acutely psychotic, and her depression was as serious as any I have ever seen in a young person. After she came out of the depression, in about forty-eight hours, some paranoid material became apparent, but what could really be seen was a desperately unhappy adolescent with an undifferentiated psychotic reaction. I do not yet know, nor will I know for a while, the basis of her reaction, but her condition was not such as to justify electroshock treatment, presumably suitable on the basis of the category in which she had been placed. This is not the place to discuss electroshock treatment; the point to be made here is that in this situation, even though the diagnosis was probably in error,

11

the pattern of response was set once the patient was categorized and would have been carried through but for the request of the family for another opinion.

In such patterns of response some of the considerations are to be seen that lead me to state that the formulation of crisis theory has given us a way to take another kind of look at ourselves and our services— a new way to relate needs to service and to relate the principles of treatment to the principles of prevention. Crisis theory can provide a useful scaffolding for a large gamut of problems, as can the newer concepts of primary prevention and the public health model. This model seems to me to be of the utmost significance to our whole field; it encompasses case-finding, working with people before they are in crisis and become ill, making our limited services available to cut down the pool of people at risk, and then beginning to deal concurrently with the people drawn out of this pool who are, in fact, in crisis. I see as a goal in our joint fields of service a moving back of crisis intervention to an earlier point in individual experience. We started out with interventions with very sick people; then we moved to people in the kind of crisis in which the problems are on the borderline between being subacute and being chronic. Now I see us moving in social psychiatry and its allied fields into an area further back—to those people who are minimally involved in psychological difficulties, or currently not involved, but who are at risk of serious illness. Crisis is the thermometer that measures the fever in their systems, and crisis theory helps us to learn promptly what constitutes appropriate early treatment or preventive measures. I see such a use of crisis theory as the most significant development to be expected of the next several decades in community mental health work.

WHAT IS A CRISIS?

Before we launch into a discussion of crisis theory, a brief working definition of crisis is in order. For the purpose of this discussion, crisis means simply a disequilibrium, an unstable system—using system in the formal sense in which it is used when we speak of general systems theory. The system may involve a personality, a family, an urban community, or many other entities. When that system is upset—when it is out of balance—there is a crisis.

Having established a working definition, I shall reverse the usual order: before discussing crisis theoretically, I shall start by citing some specific examples of crisis and discussing them individually and informally; then I shall present a theoretical framework and some generalizations.

ILLUSTRATIONS OF CRISIS

I should like to cite several points that should be kept in mind as the cases are reviewed.

Before one can intervene in a crisis, one has to enter the system that is in disequilibrium. It is important to think of crisis intervention in terms of the level of entry and the leverage provided by the entry. Then key questions must be answered: Where, at what level, and how does one enter the system? At what level does one work? What are the choices of opportunity for intervening? What factors are working in one's favor, and what factors are going against one? What are the possibilities for doing anything useful for the client by intervening? Would it be better to stay out of the system? And—of critical importance—when should one terminate intervention and how?

A Developmental Crisis

A moderately attractive woman in her mid-thirties, who had been teaching in a high school in a small community, entered overseas service for a philanthropic organization. She had done extremely well in her teaching career, and although her life had set into a somewhat rigid pattern from which she rarely escaped, her work gave her considerable satisfaction. She was motivated to seek overseas service by the fact that her childhood and religious training had been pervaded by an ideal of service to other human beings that her job did not satisfy. She had a highly successful two-year term of service living in a culture very different from her own. During that period she discovered some aspects of herself that in some ways gratified her and in some ways embarrassed her. She found, for example, that she had sexual feelings and that it was possible to give those feelings some expression in a way that was appropriate in the culture in which she found herself. She had a meaningful sexual relationship while overseas, which terminated of necessity when she returned home. I saw her in a routine termination interview designed for talking over her overseas experience— what it had meant to her, what the living conditions had been like, how her colleagues had gotten along together, and so on. Suddenly, I was confronted with an acute crisis growing out of her sexual experience. She expressed the crisis thus: "How do I put the genie back in the bottle? What do I do now? I could accept this thing five thousand miles away, but it's pretty hard to accept in the small town where I teach."

She was a person who had come into my office—and notice, I said *person*, not *patient*—with a real crisis in her life: Having discovered her sexual feelings in a culture in which she could find an appropriate expression for them, how was she to adjust to another culture, albeit her own, in which she could not? Then came my own questions. At what level should I work with her? Clearly the problem could be approached at many different psychodynamic levels. To what extent should I reassure her? If I reassured her, what else would she need?

The case resolved itself with relative ease. I let her talk freely and then guided her to talk of a host of feelings—not only the sexual feelings that had become manifest while she was overseas. I pointed out that she had not received a mandate to go out hunting; that she simply had some new-found feelings she could use or not use; that it was equally appropriate *not* to use them as to use them; that, essentially, she had some choices to make; that she had the capacity for making choices; and that as long as she acted in a way congruent with her own feelings, the choices would work out for her. I did not say, "I want to see you next Tuesday at three o'clock." I said, "When you feel you have something to say, come in and we'll talk

13

about it." I saw her again, at her request, about four weeks later. She had gone back to her school district and was making a good adjustment; yet she was finding her life in her small town somewhat too confining for her new motor. She had to race it somewhere, and so she had begun to build a social life that provided an opportunity for the expression of a variety of interests. I saw her once more some four or five weeks later. She wanted to talk about her own situation and my way of approaching her crisis, because, she said, she encountered youngsters in her teaching who were in the same kind of crisis constantly.

Whether this young woman's choices of action were right or wrong is not germane. The point is that all the elements of crisis in a normal human being were present in the case. This person's equilibrium was upset by a completely new kind of cultural experience, and a new dimension in her own feelings was added. When she moved back into her own culture, she was confronted by the kinds of questions that it is usual to ask under such circumstances.

A Medical Crisis

A man in his middle fifties awoke one Saturday morning to find blood in his sputum. An intelligent man, he called his physician for guidance at once. He was hospitalized, and immediately a large mass was seen in one lung; he had a bronchogenic carcinoma.

This man had been an active head of his family, but he was quickly rendered incapable of that function not only by the lung damage but also eventually by cerebral damage as well. His wife did not know where to turn. The physician, of course, was not equipped to help her handle the family's multitudinous problems with respect to rearing the children, getting financial help, and generally mobilizing its resources; wisely, he referred the wife to a family agency, in the hope that the agency and he, working together, could find some solutions. The wife could not get an appointment for ten days, however, during which time the husband underwent pulmonary surgery; in addition, he was scheduled for cranial surgery. The wife persisted and did see a worker; the worker indicated that she really did not know what could be done because she was not sure what the wife wanted done.

Certainly the social worker was correct about the wife's indecision. Clearly this woman was in a crisis and did not know what was going on within herself and her family. The marriage itself was in crisis. It had never been a markedly satisfying one for her, and she felt guilt about her husband's illness and ambivalence about what she hoped would be the outcome. Furthermore, the marital crisis was complicated by her extreme dependence on her husband, both emotionally and practically. The family's manifest crisis centered around the problems of financing the husband's care and the needs of the wife and children, particularly in relation to finding new patterns for living without the guidance of the head of the family. The social worker tried to tap the emotional aspect of the wife's crisis, to help her understand her feelings first of all. But the wife refused to meet the worker on that level, and the worker gave up altogether.

Carcinoma does not wait for willingness to explore psychodynamics any more than it waits for an agency's convenience in granting an appointment. I believe that the social worker, although she was right in feeling that the wife needed help at the emotional level, should have intervened at any level at which the wife would respond; she should have attempted to work out the most pressing practical issues, offered the wife reassurance and support with respect to the marital crisis, and waited for an appropriate moment to go into the psychodynamics of the situation. One has to meet people where they want to be met, not where one thinks they ought to be met.

A Marital Crisis

Some years ago a member of the house staff of a hospital called me in a panic and in truly acute pain. His wife had just left him. She had left surreptitiously during his absence from home and taken with her all their household possessions and their car.

I had seen the couple a few times previously, and I had not been able to understand clearly what they had been trying to say, particularly the wife. She kept saying, in effect, "He's not a good husband. He doesn't come home when he's on duty at night." Her message was, of course, a conflicting one, since physicians who are on duty at night remain in their hospitals. She also said, "He's not companionable; he wants to read his medical books." The wife's second message was not an unfamiliar one, but her anger was clearly disproportionate to the situation, at least as it came through to me.

When approached by the young husband after his wife's departure, I chose to intervene exclusively at the level of reality. He was suffering an acute mourning reaction, apparently involving mixed feelings about the wife he had lost. I spent most of my time with him in discussing what he should do next and, in a guarded way, helping him handle the guilt and anxiety he felt. I was guarded in my approach because I think it important in crisis intervention to let appropriate feelings—or feelings that *may* be appropriate—flourish; stifling guilt merely delays the process of working it through. Sometimes, people are best able to handle guilt when their situation is acute, and when their whole system is in disarray.

I saw this man occasionally over a period of weeks, and he began to work through his crisis. I never saw his wife again. I believe that she was, unfortunately, a very sick young woman who could not respond to help.

A Tragedy

A man in his mid-twenties, who had an excellent school record, had had two years of foreign service in Latin America working for a private organization. During this term of service, he had done extremely well, according to reports from the people concerned. His medical record in an exceedingly perilous situation had been good, although he had used tranquilizers (moderately) and had suffered occasional attacks of a respiratory difficulty (common in the country in which he had been serving).

After termination of service, he decided he wanted more overseas experience and was interviewed by several people, including me, who serve the organization in a selection capacity. We felt he was most suitable for the post he sought in a developing country and should go ahead to do the work he wanted to do. Shortly thereafter he went to Paris. He was seen by various people there who reported that he seemed to be his usual self. He hitchhiked from Paris to southern Germany and back in about four days, which took at least some enterprise and stamina. He was seen again just before he took a plane to go to his new post. It appears that he got off the plane in the capital of the country, which was French-speaking. He could speak very little French. The place in which he intended to work was not the capital, as had been thought, but a place some four hours from it by a very rough road. Unaccompanied by any other English-speaking person, he made his way to the work site and functioned effectively—it is believed —for about two weeks. Then he came back to the capital, saw a doctor there, and was subsequently admitted to a hospital. On admission, he had malaria and, in addition, a dermatitis common among foreigners in the tropics. It appears that he was in considerable panic. As noted, he spoke little French—and he was in a French-speaking hospital. The nurses and his doctors spoke only French, and, so far as can be determined, the only person in the hospital who spoke English was a British ex-sergeant who had cirrhosis of the liver. In the hospital, the American began to make strenuous attempts, in a nonverbal way, to get help, to indicate how critically ill he was—for example, by screaming and breaking windows. Nobody paid any attention, including an American junior consular official with whom he had previously become acquainted. Finally, he was locked in his room, at which point he went into an acute psychotic episode, accompanied by hallucinations. After three or four days, in a panic, he broke a window in his second-floor room, jumped onto the porch roof below and then off the porch roof, and disappeared into the brush. He was found two and a half days later, hanging from a thorn tree.

This tragedy clearly shows the need for intervention in crisis and, particularly, the importance of early intervention, if intervention is to serve a preventive function. The outcome in this situation may be attributed to the people on the spot, who did not recognize the excessive decompensation of the man's crisis, and to the organization, which did not make sure that there were caretakers available who knew how to respond to his needs at an appropriate level. Somewhere along the line someone should have recognized the increasingly loud shouts for help that this man emitted and taken action that would have prevented the worsening of the crisis to a point at which the man could find relief from mounting tensions only in suicide.

To find all the points at which this tragedy could have been prevented, however, it is necessary to go back even further, to the recruitment phase of the story. Since I find nothing in my detailed selection data that should have red-flagged me from the psychiatric standpoint, the implication is that situational factors should have been given more careful attention. It may be dangerous to send Americans alone to a country whose language they do not know or to a country in which there are prevalent physical diseases against which they cannot be immunized; without doubt dangers are magnified if there are no sources of help reasonably nearby. A lack of primary prevention is certainly suggested in this history.

16

CRISIS THEORY DISCUSSED

Now, after the foregoing rough sketch, it seems appropriate to discuss crisis theory in a more formal way. The discussion will be derived largely from various formulations of Gerald Caplan,[2] somewhat modified as a result of our joint experience in Peace Corps work.

A discussion of crisis theory should start with a consideration of the normal individual and his emotional functioning—based on the known fact that all human beings establish an equilibrium physiochemically, neurologically, intrapsychically, extrapsychically, and socially. This equilibrium can be defined in sociological terms, in anthropological terms, or in psychodynamic terms. It does not matter, so long as we understand that all of us come to some kind of steady state, emotionally and physically. It may bring greater or less contentment with greater or less effectiveness, but it brings, at least, a continuity of identity and operation, which tends to remain relatively constant for adults. The equilibrium is dynamic, not static, however. A day-by-day chart would surely show fluctuations, probably, but not necessarily, in an arrangement specific for each individual. Viewed over time, the points, of course, would tend to flatten out and show a fairly consistent pattern of operation.

The system operates with reasonable efficiency in reference to the culture in which the individual lives. It cannot be judged independently of his culture, or subculture. Especially in dealing with people living in large, heterogeneous communities, it is essential to identify the subculture in which they operate. We can easily make the mistake of thinking that they all come from our culture, when in fact they do not. We must determine realistically what the steady state for an individual client or family is, rather than what we think it should be from our knowledge of our own subculture or sub-subculture.

What characterizes the steady state, of course, is appropriate minimal anxiety and appropriate minimal feeling of strain consistent with the usual pattern of the particular individual's feeling. In psychoanalytic terms, we talk about the availability to a person of the usual and adequate problem-solving mechanisms. Sometimes, these are called, quaintly, mechanisms of defense. But problem-solving mechanisms are more than mechanisms of defense, because mechanisms of defense are, in a way, artificial. Problem-solving mechanisms are really devices, learned over a period of time, for solving problems; they include, but are not limited to, defense mechanisms. They are used consciously, preconsciously, and unconsciously to solve our problems with relatively minimal dislocation of the self and others. They are used to keep the individual in a state of relative equilibrium with the environment with respect to his own particular patterns of reaction to that environment.

The environment, itself, of course, is also in a state of dynamic balance. Not one of us lives through a week without some jolts, but the jolts from the

2 For a comprehensive presentation, see Gerald Caplan, *Principles of Preventive Psychiatry*, Basic Books, New York, 1964.

17

environment can be handled within the flexible balance of the healthy individual. Two systems are moving, but they are moving slowly in relation to each other, and the individual ordinarily knows how to solve problems within his own culture as the environment moves past him. Sometimes events in the larger world dislocate everyone simultaneously, as did the catastrophe of November 22, 1963. Every feeling individual's sensibilities and sense of balance were jolted. People found means—in some instances, not very adequate means—of dealing with the situation: some stayed in front of the television set too long, and others stayed away from it entirely; some tried to deal with the situation by asking questions of other people, recognizing at the time that they were solving their problems by asking others how they were solving theirs.

Most people have at hand patterns of response that stand them in good stead in cases of social dislocation. I am sure, however, that we all have had patients or clients who were not able to handle the impact of the tremendous input into the environmental stress in this instance. Some of the people who had a tendency to misinterpret events became clinically paranoid. Some people who had lived in cultures in which the assassination of leaders has a profound effect on individuals reacted, not with clinical illness, but in terms specific to their earlier experiences with the same kind of situation. How one reacts to crisis depends in some measure, then, on how one is conditioned to react to crisis. And one of the serious problems in crisis intervention is shortness of time for obtaining information. We have to use the few clues provided us in a hurry by the client, supplemented by educated guesses, to determine what the crisis really means in reference to the client's background, or his pattern of crisis reaction, which has developed over a long period of time.

There are, of course, time-patterned crises in life. These are the crises that occur in the normal development of every individual. If we can believe some writers, there is a crisis at birth, but data are meager, at least so far as the infant is concerned. Some of us are familiar with the crisis of adolescence, among our clients and patients and sometimes in our own families, and we recognize that adolescence is a period in which there is no steady state, or at least no very long one; we know that trying to chase an adolescent around in order to intervene in a crisis can be a wearying experience. We are aware that marriage brings about a time of crisis, of major disequilibrium, of major change in patterns of problem-solving. The climacteric presents another kind of crisis. And the crises of aging are often very tragic ones.

Perhaps the most useful model on which to base our thinking about dealing with crisis is the normal crisis of mourning. This is an experience most of us have had to endure; we know what it is like. We know how helpless one can feel, even with reasonably good personality resources, when one is trying to work through a loss; we know about the maladaptive patterns of behavior that present themselves, until one comes to the real work of mourning.

These, then, are normal developmental crises of life. Between them and the crises illustrated earlier that may be called accidental crises, there is a

18

group of transient states of disequilibrium that cannot be properly called crises though they are significantly uncomfortable for the person involved. In these situations, the person faces a problem outside his usual problem-solving and coping methods, a situation that upsets his current functioning. The upset lasts a fairly brief time. He approaches the problem using his usual coping mechanisms. They may be ineffective or only partially effective; even so the period of tension, during which he is seeking new patterns to resolve the problem, is not excessive. In a sense, the person cannot come to grips with the problem with both hands, but, at least, he can hold onto it with one hand while he figures out what to do with the other, so that he keeps in contact with himself and with the problem as he goes about trying to solve it.

Psychiatrists and social workers are seldom called upon in such cases, except gratuitously in the course of a treatment situation. The physician, on the contrary, is familiar with such states of disequilibrium in the course of a physical illness, and so is the caseworker in a general hospital. From a technical standpoint, it is important that intervention be minimal in such situations, because jumping in precipitately amounts to robbing the person of a meaningful experience, of a chance to gain something for himself through his own efforts, something that will make him more comfortable the next time he meets a similar kind of problem.

Such transient states become troublesome when they develop in a patient or client in psychological treatment if the connection with the current treatment situation is not entirely clear. One has to decide whether or not the disequilibrium is outside the treatment situation and, if it is, to leave it alone. But one must recognize the risks involved. One can be wrong; the disequilibrium may indeed be connected with the treatment situation. One has to balance this risk against that of robbing the patient, by intervening drastically, of the chance to work out the problem himself. In short, then, intervention in states of transient disequilibrium may not be helpful or useful and may, in fact, be damaging.

Real crisis, as distinct from transient states of disequilibrium, is a disequilibrium that persists over a relatively long period of time. It does not last for years, because people cannot stay in crisis for years, but it lasts for weeks, rather than for the hours or days of a transient disequilibrium. To the person in crisis, everything about himself, his life, and his problems looms large. His usual readjusting and problem-solving forces are not successful within the usual or expected time range. The hope that "it will be better tomorrow" does not materialize. In fact, tomorrow is actually worse, because the daylight does not bring with it a rush of problem-solving as usual. There is a prolonged inconsistency of behavior patterns in crisis, but eventually an equilibrium is established. It may be based on a pattern of adaptation that is significantly different from the person's former patterns; it may be healthier than a former pattern, or it may be far less healthy. The problem of the crisis has to be solved, however, and it will be solved—either by coping and learning or by regressing and retreating, but the solution will be reached in a new way.

Rarely does crisis arise exclusively from a single major event, except in

19

cases of death or serious illness. Crisis usually presents itself as a series of smaller crises; when put together, they are all parts of one major upheaval. Gerald Caplan states: "The significance of a crisis is in its temporal telescoping of development. [It develops in a telescopic way.] Major alterations in pattern may occur in a relatively short period and may subsequently remain stable for a long time [either in a very good or in an unhealthy kind of way]." [3]

A typical state of crisis may be characterized as follows: The problems at hand are too big, too novel, or too important to be dealt with by resources immediately available (certainly this was true in the case of the young man who committed suicide overseas and that of the family faced with the father's bronchogenic carcinoma). No coping mechanisms are available within the time available for solution of the problems. The problems can be neither met nor side-stepped. In themselves, they present a real danger to the individual, or they jeopardize a major need gratification in some way. The tension resulting either from danger or from frustration mounts, and it may threaten the integrity of the self.

Four stages of crisis development have been described:

In the first stage there is a rise in tension caused by the emergence of a problem or of problems. During this stage there is an attempt to evoke the usual problem-solving techniques. If these are effective within a short time, the crisis is no longer a crisis.

In the second stage there is a failure of the habitual coping devices and a period of upset and ineffectuality. For example, the doctor discussed previously was having a difficult time making his rounds and doing his work because he was so preoccupied with deciding what to do about his runaway wife. Such a failure gives rise to anxiety, helplessness, fear, guilt, and shame, and it finally leads to an attempt to mobilize others to help.

In the third stage there is a further rise in tension, which stimulates action, one hopes. It is the stimulus for the mobilization of the internal resources both of the person in crisis and his family and of external resources, to develop some kind of emergency problem-solving mechanism. For this third stage, four kinds of approach toward finding new problem-solving mechanisms have been described.

First, the person may attack the problem in a trial-and-error way. For example, he may identify with a care-giving person, either amateur or professional; ask, "What would you do?"; and then try the suggested solution. Or he may seek to identify with others who have been in similar situations and then attempt their solutions.

Second, he may redefine the problem, possibly excluding parts of it that seem impossible of solution. In doing so, the person, in a sense, deals with a small piece of the problem as a symbol of the whole. For this approach, normal mourning of certain subcultures can be seen as a model: The energy invested by the family in mourning in solving the problem of feeding other mourners does part of the work of mourning, or at least makes it possible

---

[3] Gerald Caplan, *Principles of Preventive Psychiatry*, Basic Books, New York, 1964, p. 39.

for the family to detach energy from mourning itself and deal with this real problem later when it is more capable of doing so.

A person in another kind of crisis may do very much the same thing. The doctor in the illustrative case given earlier did so when his wife left him. Ordinarily, he uses a fairly intellectual approach to problem-solving: he looks over the whole problem, breaks it down into its component parts, and proceeds to work them out, one at a time, in a systematic way. In the crisis of his wife's departure, this method failed him: the problem was so overwhelming that he simply could not take hold of it in its entirety, could not see its separate parts, and could not understand the relationship of the parts to the whole. He removed from its context one part, the car, which was half his and which his wife had taken, and focused all his attention on it; he tried to deal with this part as if it were the whole problem. I recognized that I had to deal with the whole problem, but I had to enter the situation where I could, where he wanted to focus his attention. We spent considerable time discussing the practical matter of the car theft. Once this problem was solved by his decision to let her keep the car, he was able to give up some of his ties with his wife. Thus, he began to face the issue of separation from her by dealing first with a problem that was a symbol of the separation. Though he was never actually conscious of his substitution of the part for the whole, working on that selected part of the whole sustained him until he could begin consciously to tackle the whole problem. Intervention in the crisis as he had chosen to approach it saved him from being presented with all its implications in one short period of time, but, at the same time, it prepared him to deal more effectively with the whole problem later on.

Third, a person may approach his problem in this third stage by way of limited regression. Limited regression, like any other kind of therapeutically induced regression, permits a rebuilding. The situation is analogous, I believe, to what happens when a person has active tuberculosis. He may first fight very hard and deny that he is going to be out of action for a while. One tries to help him see the crisis as a medical crisis, one that will necessitate his being out of action. Eventually, he says, in effect, "Okay, I give up." But the healthy person does not give up for all time; he gives up only for a while. He heals his lung, and he heals himself in the sense of accepting his body image. Then he begins to build again.

Fourth, a person may approach his problem through a realignment of his social group, though doing so is not always a separate approach; it may be combined with the third approach. The group—frequently either directly or indirectly persuaded to do so by the individual, but sometimes of its own volition—simply accommodates the individual in his altered state and makes a place for him in its functioning. Thus, he establishes a kind of equilibrium with it, which eases his crisis, although the actual problems of the crisis may remain unsolved and a new crisis may be imminent.

In the fourth stage of crisis—which we hope to prevent—the problem remains unsolved and unavoidable, the burden increases to the breaking point, and some kind of personality decompensation takes place. There may be symptom formation: for example, physical symptoms like the reactivation, or the activation, of a peptic ulcer; an attack of ulcerative colitis in a young person; an incapacitating migraine or backache; or anything that takes the person in crisis out of the firing line. Or there may be a dissociative state of some sort or an acute depression.

As an illustration, a woman under my care handled a crisis in her family magnificently, about which I felt very happy. Then she went back to her habitual pattern of regressive depression, into the severest depression of her sixty years. Now this pattern of recurring depression is fixed. I do not know whether or not the fixation of this pattern could have been prevented, but the case points up the necessity to watch time sequences in dealing with crises. Just as a pitcher can sometimes pitch the ninth inning and then have his arm go limp, so people mobilize their resources, appear to solve a problem, and then go limp all over.

The factors that influence the outcomes of crises are many. As has been suggested, there is a specific kind of vulnerability built into people by previous crises and their solutions to them. There is a link-up of the problems of the present to those of the past, one aspect of which has been recently explored by a doctoral candidate at the University of Pennsylvania.[4] He attempts to correlate adult depressions with separations from important people in the past life of the individual. His hypothesis, of course, is that depressions have to do with separations; that for people who have previously experienced separations and not solved them successfully, a separation, whether actual or symbolic, that precipitates a depression in later life constitutes a greater crisis than it would have if the earlier separation had been weathered more successfully. The data are somewhat ambiguous; nevertheless, if one thinks about the depressed persons one has known, it appears that the idea is at least worth pursuing.

Previous patterning, then, is extremely important; though each crisis is novel, it has in it elements of a previous crisis, and a person's previous experience in crisis is an important determinant of the handling of a new one. The outcome also depends on bodily health, on concomitant pressures, on the availability of external help, on the state of the person's defenses, and on his actual and potential pattern of communication with those around him.

There is a large culture-specific factor in crisis, because what is acceptable in one culture or subculture is not acceptable in another. In some families an illegitimate pregnancy is an enormous crisis; in others an illegitimate pregnancy is not a crisis at all. Not only the specific event, however, but also the values attached to it historically by the social group and by its antecedent generations become part of the pattern. Thus, a complex series of events occurs; the social system is moving around the person in crisis while his system is also in movement. There is a real play of forces between what goes on within the individual and what goes on within the environment. Moreover, there is often a reinforcement of previously introjected values, which may be neurotic or inappropriate. The person may say, "I'm

---

[4] See Aaron T. Beck, Brij B. Sethi, and Robert W. Tuthill, "Childhood Bereavement and Adult Depression," *Archives of General Psychiatry*, Vol. IX, September 1963, pp. 295–302.

not very good, but I'll really get on," or he may think, "I'm no good at all," depending on earlier identifications. And either attitude may be the salient problem that person is facing.

The amount of misinformation a person in crisis can collect from those around him is fairly substantial. Since we, as crisis interveners, are not with our people as much as their families are, very often we have to choose as the point of intervention, not the client or patient, but someone else in the social system. The social system is the locale of the major push toward maladaptive techniques—and when we point up choices to the individual in crisis, we may be indicating courses of action that he actually cannot take.

The impact of the social system can be clearly seen in the following illustration.

A doctor friend telephoned me recently and said: "I have a sixteen-year-old girl in my office who is pregnant and unmarried. She is crying, hysterical. I think her pregnancy should be terminated. Her parents are here, and they agree. Will you see her, and will you write a letter?" I agreed to see her, but said that my decision about writing a letter would have to wait. Early the next morning there came into my office a well-developed young woman, almost seventeen years of age, from a mobile upper-middle-class family. There seemed to be no doubt that she was pregnant. I learned that the prospective father was a twenty-one-year-old college senior. The girl alleged that she was in love with him, and he, apparently, was in love with her. It became increasingly clear to me that this girl did not want her pregnancy terminated and that having it terminated would have constituted the grossest kind of intrusion, an imposition of values alien to the actual situation. The girl was not really in a state of crisis, nor was the potential father. When I talked with the boy, he said: "Look, this is easy; we'll get married. If I have to drop out of school to support all of us, I'll be glad to." The girl wanted to marry him, too. It was the girl's mother who was in a state of crisis. When I talked with her, she said, "But it will kill Grandfather!" I saw my role here as requiring me to say: "I'm sorry, but Grandfather isn't the problem. If you can handle your feelings, you can help Grandfather handle his."

In this case the crucial issue for me was identification of the point of intervention, the base of leverage, in the crisis situation—and so it frequently is. Once the proper point of entry is found, the rest of the intervention flows fairly naturally. The tension for the intervener lies between his introduction to the crisis situation and his determination of the mode of entry or of whether entry should be made at all.

It is often necessary to define very carefully the boundaries between the person in crisis and those around him who are trying to help him. He is likely to scatter himself widely in the midst of crisis, and we must be able to help him regather himself, to help him retrieve his right to work out his own problems according to his own situation and his own needs. This is not always easy to do. The person may blame himself, or he may project blame to others. All of us have had clients or patients who adjust to crisis by dislocating everyone in the environment; they solve their problems simply by projecting their trouble onto those around them. Then they stand calm and

23

happy in the midst of the storm, while everyone else is screaming. It may appear that the crisis is solved, but all that has been accomplished is the setting in motion of a circular reaction. The feedback problem has not been solved; soon everybody in the surrounding group will be very angry, and the new crisis may be considerably worse than the original one.

In other words, we cannot retreat to our offices with our single patient or client and lock the door, because even if the other members of the family do not follow us in physically, they will be there with us. Consequently, we have to understand the social network of the person in crisis. But we cannot derive our understanding of it from him alone; he is the least likely to understand it.

As in going into any social system, we must get information about the family, its resources, its alliances, and its power groupings. We must know who is allied with whom, who is doing what to whom, and with what. What are the nature and quality of the family's communication? What is inevitable and cannot be changed? What *can* be changed? We must remember that the family can give absolution, reassurance, or consolation; it can do a great many things for the individual, or a great many things to him, including driving him to suicide. The point to be emphasized is that in a crisis situation, since the crisis is at least partially externally determined, with respect to both cause and outcome, the family (or whatever group the patient or client lives in) becomes equal in importance to him in the intervener's efforts to help. Without answers to many environmental questions, we lack the resources we need for effective intervention.

In the case of the pregnant unmarried girl outlined earlier, I might have made the same judgment—that the pregnancy should not be terminated—whether or not I had interviewed the mother and prospective father. But I do not think I could have done anything to help the person primarily in need of help. If this girl had gone on then to have a termination of her pregnancy, a real intrapsychic crisis would have occurred, which would have been much harder to handle than the original problem.

From our standpoint as interveners, a real difficulty arises from the necessity to make important decisions quickly—where to get into the crisis situation; how to confront it; whether to help the individual take positive steps within the situation in order to master it, to resign himself to it, in effect, or to delay tension by withdrawing from it. Human beings do not like ambiguity. In many critical situations, however, there is no way to deal with ambiguity except to help the person, his family, and perhaps even his society to live with it. If a son is missing in action, one cannot dissipate the ambiguity by asking the Secretary of Defense to send a telegram announcing his death or by insisting that he is alive. If a man is told that he will be laid off from work but not told when, one cannot make decisions on the basis of a known date. These particular problems exemplify the ambiguity typical of many kinds of crisis and point up the fact that crisis intervention should take place as early as possible in order to avoid ambiguity and its concomitant build-up of dangerous tensions; if avoidance of ambiguity is impossible, intervention should be directed toward helping the individual in crisis live with ambiguity so that his tension may be lessened.

One of the implications of crisis intervention that Caplan has emphasized in Peace Corps work should be borne in mind. This is the concept—developed by Caplan, although visible in its early beginnings in Erich Lindemann's work [5]—that a person is more susceptible to influence, good or bad, at times of crisis than at other times in his life; what Caplan calls the "leverage" in the system is greater. It is possible, therefore, through effective crisis intervention, to help the individual find relatively healthier methods of problem-solving and coping than he had before and to do so in less time than would be required under noncritical circumstances. Conversely, if a poor job of intervention is done, or no job at all, the harm is correspondingly greater. But, again, time is an element that cannot be overemphasized. One of the most important contributions to crisis theory in the past decade, and certainly in the past five years, is the development of the idea that intervention must be immediate. It must not await the convenience of the intervener. It must occur when the person is in crisis, when he begins not only to mobilize his own resources but also to solicit and to mobilize help from others. There is no time for the leisurely interview; we must find a point of maximum leverage and then move into action.

Every year I tell a group of first-year psychiatric residents that they can learn enough about a patient in twenty minutes, on intake at a psychiatric hospital, to enable them to make certain important decisions. Initially they spend the twenty minutes asking so many questions that the patient really has little chance to talk. Then I must help them see that if they ask fewer questions and listen carefully, they will learn a great deal more in a very brief time. The problem lies in wanting more information than we are likely to get from people in crisis if we restrict ourselves to traditional therapeutic methods. Dealing with people in crisis requires a certain rethinking of our methods and a certain flexibility—a willingness and ability to shift suddenly from a therapeutic approach to a purely information-getting approach and back again, if necessary. Questions must be asked, of course, but they must be key questions, and it may be necessary often to interrupt the patient or client to bring him back to the task of accumulating the data needed for making decisions. Moreover, one must not hesitate to use ancillary sources of information.

Crisis intervention makes heavy demands on the intervener to shift gears constantly, to innovate in some ways and to retain a relatively classic approach in others. We must do so, moreover, without any real guideposts except our own knowledge of humanity and our own technical abilities, which means that supervision must be heavily depended on. In crisis intervention supervision must be geared, not to the question "Did you do the right thing technically?" but to such queries as "Did you do what you did at the right time?" "Could you have acted with less information?" "Should you have waited for more information?" and so on.

[5] Stanley Cobb and Erich Lindemann, "Neuropsychiatric Observations" (from Symposium on The Management of the Cocoanut Grove Burns at the Massachusetts General Hospital), *Annals of Surgery*, Vol. CXVII, June 1943, pp. 814–24, and Erich Lindemann, "Symptomatology and Management of Acute Grief," *The American Journal of Psychiatry*, Vol. CI, September 1944, pp. 141–48.

SOME SPECIAL CONSIDERATIONS

Termination of Intervention

There is no more crucial aspect of timing in crisis intervention than the timing of termination. Again, there are no hard and fast rules; each case must be decided on its own merits. The analogy with the physically ill patient is obvious: when he begins to be able to take care of his own needs, he should be allowed to do so, no matter how slowly, as long as he does not risk injuring himself. So also when the person in crisis shows the first signs of being able to stand on his own, the intervener should allow him to try it, and he should withdraw as soon as he sees that his client or patient is functioning with reasonable effectiveness and without damaging himself or others.

The relationship between the intervener and the individual in crisis must not be allowed to become a long-term therapeutic one. The people we help in crisis are abnormally dependent at that time. Their resources are unequal to the demands of the current situation and they seek outside help. To continue to give help after the person has developed the necessary means for handling the situation is to prolong dependency and encourage sickness. In the case of the young woman who, on returning from service abroad, was in a crisis involving her newly discovered sexual feelings, I made no specific arrangements for seeing her a second time. I did not want her to think of herself as a patient or a sick person and therefore put off the choices and decisions that led eventually to the healthy outcome of her crisis.

Significant Others and Skilled Amateurs

When the individual in crisis reaches a point at which he signals for help, various people in the environment may be stimulated to respond. These people are appropriately termed "the significant others" in his situation. Of course, these significant others may be very good amateur caretakers, or they may be very bad ones. In such a situation there are many pitfalls for the amateur: he may enjoy being leaned on, for example, and he may allow, or encourage, the person who is in crisis to lean on him more than he should.

Most patients and clients have sought help from one or more such amateur caretakers before reaching a professional helping person. In a small community, the amateur may be the corner grocer, who probably hears about more problems, and hears about them sooner, than do psychiatrists and social workers. He may be a janitor, for in many communities the person designated as the gatekeeper becomes a most significant other. Then there are family physicians, clergymen, teachers, policemen, and so on through a long list. They may be professionally trained for their respective fields, but they are for the most part amateurs in the psychological skills needed for good caretaking in crisis.

The initial leverage in crisis intervention frequently lies with amateur caretakers, and so, then, does potential for prevention if they are trained to be *skilled amateurs*, as they are called in the Peace Corps. In the Peace Corps significant others are trained to be skilled amateurs in crisis intervention, with the result that it is not necessary to keep a large staff of psychiatrists, psychologists, or caseworkers in the field. Rather, other personnel, both administrative and medical, are taught to function effectively as psychological caretakers, and the volunteers themselves are taught to give each other psychological first aid, as I shall describe later.

It must be borne in mind that the capability and role of the skilled amateur are very different from those of the professional intervener. The skilled amateur does not have the professional's reservoir of technical skill, or necessarily his flexibility, or his ability to handle a wide range of problems; moreover, after a time, he uses himself up in a given situation because he lacks the professional caretaker's capacity for self-renewal. Nevertheless, he can be an extremely useful person, in any society, especially in filling critical lacunae caused by the manpower shortage. All one has to do is go into any mental hospital to see what effective caretaking is provided by certain aides. Everyone will tell you that they are not supposed to be providing psychological aid and that they cannot, but the fact remains that they *do*—which is not to say that skilled amateurs will replace professionals.

TWO PROGRAMS OF CRISIS INTERVENTION [6]

Making use of crisis theory, there are a number of ways of designing consultation procedures to improve the skills of the amateur intervener, the intervener who has not been professionally trained in psychological skills.

A Program in a Rural Area

In northern Minnesota in an area covering several very large counties having a population of about 90,000, a program has been set up that makes planned use of amateur caretakers. It began when a young psychiatrist named Frank Kiesler came into the area when there were available no psychiatric or casework services whatever. He was immediately deluged with psychiatric referrals. Clearly, he could not handle the needs of such a big area on an individual basis. He decided to use crisis theory as his starting point. He set up a team consisting of himself, a social worker, and a clinical psychologist. Then they began answering the telephone. They dealt directly with what they called the firing-line manpower in the area: the physicians; the clergy; the school personnel, including nurses; the welfare agency workers; and the public health nurses—in short, everyone who was likely to respond to calls for help in crisis at a professional or semiprofessional level. These amateur caretakers were told that if they wished, the team would help them with individual crises and perhaps teach them some of the techniques of handling crises in general.

Team members see few clients or patients, and those only as a last resort. They make use of the therapeutic potential of amateur interveners, and they identify, through their communication circuit, persons in need of more specialized help. Kiesler does not see the plan as a complete solution to the area's needs for psychological service, and, of course, it is not. But what he is doing is backing up the people on the firing line in dealing with crises

---

[6] The programs are described as observed in 1964.

and providing them with an identification model to use in dealing with the ultimate patient or client. He is teaching the crisis intervention skills and providing the consultation that make significant others skilled amateur interveners. He has found, at least, a partial solution to the problem of compensating for the critical shortage of skilled manpower, at one tenth of the usual cost of conventional services.

The Peace Corps Program

The Peace Corps has a unique, but broadly relevant, crisis intervention and consultation program. It began when the Congress, believing that the project would attract "a lot of kooks," insisted that all volunteers must be screened psychiatrically. Although it seemed logistically impossible, every one of the first seven or eight hundred volunteers was examined individually for psychiatric clearance. Two facts emerged: First, there were not many psychotics among the applicants—in fact, practically none; second, the psychiatrists did not know a great deal about interviewing normal people for selection purposes. It was decided eventually that the individual psychiatric interview was not making maximal use of psychiatric manpower and skill, and, furthermore, there simply were not enough psychiatrists available to handle the growing load of applicants on an individual basis. Nevertheless, the requirement remained that every volunteer must be cleared psychiatrically.

The psychiatrists who were serving at the time as consultants to the Peace Corps had to intervene in what was, in effect, a Peace Corps crisis. And a different kind of program was set up.

Now, one psychiatrist for each fifty-five trainees spends one day a week at the training site. He goes to classes with the trainees, attends their meetings and bull sessions, and joins them at meals; he interacts with them and gets to know them in a variety of ways, observing their behavior under all conditions of the training situation, a situation that replicates as closely as possible the stresses and crises of the service situation. Moreover, the objective of the screening process has been broadened: an effort is made to learn not only which trainees *are not* suited psychologically for service but also which trainees *are* especially suited for service, and in what ways and for what particular kinds of jobs. The psychiatrists' conclusions are based on continuing observation and on study of various data rather than on individual interviews, which are used only under certain special circumstances, for about 20 percent of the trainees. A recommendation is made for or against selection for service for every trainee.

The Peace Corps crisis of the manpower shortage vis-à-vis the demand for clearance was solved. At the same time, the psychiatrists were able to learn a great deal about normal functioning, with the result that a far more useful mode of selection evolved. Furthermore, psychiatric manpower was released for use in various aspects of training, for example, helping the trainees prepare psychologically for overseas service and helping them deal with the personal crises that inevitably arise in the face of a novel and stressful training experience.

Following this phase in the development of the selection and training

28

program, a few of the other psychiatric consultants began to go into the field to see how things were going, particularly with respect to the emotional support the volunteers were receiving overseas. Among other things, the consultants learned that they could make use of crisis for training amateurs in giving psychological aid to those in difficulty. They drew into their orbit the Peace Corps physician stationed in the host country and responsible for the health of the volunteers there, the director of the program there, his associate, his administrative staff, the volunteer group leaders, and the volunteers themselves.

All these people had been trained before they went into the field in various techniques of giving psychological help to others under the specific circumstances of field service. Their somewhat theoretical training was amplified by actual experience as they intervened in various crises. When they were unable to manage crises unaided, consultative help was available to them from a closely linked chain extending from the individual volunteer in the field to the psychiatric consultant staff in Washington. This chain was designed not to remove intervention from the skilled amateur but rather to help him manage the immediate crisis and learn from it how to deal more effectively with future crises. At the same time, of course, training stressed alertness to signs of need for specialized, direct professional intervention.

Following is an illustration of the way in which crisis intervention operates in the Peace Corps.

In a Latin American country a volunteer developed a dermatitis that caused him psychological as well as physical distress. His fellow-workers supported him as much as they could. They lightened his work load, and they allowed him to ventilate his feelings. When they felt they had done all they could, they asked the volunteer group leader to take over. He gave similar support, but he soon realized that more was needed, and so he sent the young man to the Peace Corps physician in the area. The physician treated the skin lesions, but he recognized serious emotional concomitants with which he could deal only on a temporary, supportive basis. He sought help from a Washington psychiatrist who happened to be visiting the area. This psychiatrist sent the volunteer back to the United States for psychiatric care. The psychiatrist to whom the volunteer was ultimately referred felt that an acute psychosis might have developed except for the intervention of the persons all along the line who recognized not only that the young man needed emergency emotional support but also that he needed specialized care.

In short, the Peace Corps program for emotional support in the field tries to utilize crises as opportunities for the prevention of serious mental disturbance, for helping the individual in crisis to grow rather than regress, for making limited manpower maximally effective, and for allowing the intervener, particularly the amateur in giving psychological help, to "learn by doing." [7]

[7] Robert L. Leopold and Leonard J. Duhl, "New Frontiers in Psychiatry: The Peace Corps," *Psychiatric Studies and Projects*, Vol. II, January 1964, pp. 1–9.

SUMMARY

Defined in its simplest terms, crisis is a disequilibrium brought about in any system—in this discussion, a personality—by an encounter with problems so large, so novel, or so important that the usual problem-solving and coping methods employed by the system are not adequate for dealing with them. Since no one can live permanently in a state of disequilibrium, the crisis always subsides, but its outcome may be either healthy or unhealthy: that is, the individual emerging from a crisis adopts behavior patterns that are different from his previous ones, and whether they are healthy or unhealthy patterns depends on a number of factors. A major one of these is the kind of help he receives from persons who respond to his need, for according to a major tenet of crisis theory, persons are more susceptible to influence, good or bad, when they are in crisis than at other times in their lives. Thus, intervention in crisis has extremely significant implications for prevention as well as for treatment. By helping to solve the immediate problems of the crisis, intervention may forestall serious developments; it may also actually help the individual in crisis to enlarge his resources for dealing with future problems. By the same token, poor help, or no help at all, may drive him into patterns of stagnation and regression that will limit significantly his capacity to deal with future problems.

In order to intervene effectively in crisis, the helping person must gain entry into the social system of the individual, for no crisis may be considered a thing apart from the society in which it occurs. The point of entry must be one that gives the intervener the greatest possible leverage in the system. Frequently, it is found not in the individual in crisis but in someone who wields significant influence in his group. The intervener must find out who that someone is, as well as many other vital data about the individual's social group and its functioning. Gathering such information by traditional therapeutic methods takes a great deal of time. But time is at a premium in crisis, for there is always a rise of tension as the crisis develops, and as tension increases, the risk increases that pathological means will be sought to relieve it before the intervener is able to help the person find effective and creative means. Thus, a major problem for the intervener is to acquire quickly the information he needs as a basis for making important decisions that cannot be deferred. He may have to resort to methods for getting this information that differ considerably from his usual ones. It is not necessary that he ask a great many questions; rather, he must ask a few key questions that invite detailed answers. It may be necessary for him to interrupt the patient frequently to keep him from wandering too far afield. In addition, the intervener must not hesitate to make unusually free use of ancillary sources of information.

The intervener must meet the person in crisis where he wants to be met, rather than where the intervener thinks he should be met. Otherwise, he may not be met at all. For example, if the person wants to focus on the immediate realities of his situation, the intervener must direct attention there, no matter how keenly he feels a need to explore the psychodynamic implications of the situation. Or if the person in crisis wants to focus on a part of his problem, the intervener must give him time to work out a solution of that part as a symbolic solution of the whole, in preparation for facing the whole.

In general, it may be said that the problems one deals with in crisis intervention are in some ways different from those of therapy, and in some ways similar. They move faster, are often more superficial, and, at least initially, are more task-pitched and reality-pitched. The intervener's role must be clearly defined, and an attempt must be made to help the individual in crisis understand his role in relation to the problems at hand. Though the usual problems of transference and countertransference arise, they cannot be dealt with exhaustively in a crisis situation. The intervener may need to reach some understanding of possible negative reactions to a client or patient, but he must put aside any hostility as best he can in favor of immediacy, appropriateness, and continuity of care.

The termination of intervention is of the utmost importance. No one has the right, by allowing the intervention situation to develop into a long-standing therapeutic relationship, to deprive an individual of his right to utilize the crisis as an opportunity for growth. The intervener should withdraw as soon as the client or patient demonstrates his capacity for functioning effectively on his own.

Not all crisis intervention is the work of professional persons. The significant others who respond to early calls for help are apt to be persons who have not been trained in giving psychological help, although they may be professionals in other areas. These amateurs can be trained to be skilled amateurs, utilizing crisis preventively by providing for the earliest possible intervention and at the same time conserving professional manpower.

CONCLUSION

Crisis theory constitutes a formal explication of much that has been well known to all of us for many years. But it presents us with an opportunity—in a society beset by problems of size and complexity, institutionalization, specialization, and professionalization in the face of ever-increasing shortages of professional manpower—to take an entirely new look at ourselves and our services, at the relationship between needs and services, and at ways of relating the principles of treatment to those of prevention. It provides a scaffolding on which to develop an approach to the problems of mental health and illness—an approach that seeks to provide immediate, realistic human responses to current and realistic human needs; strives for maximal utilization of professional manpower through the training of immediately available amateur caretakers; and stresses prevention and treatment as concurrent processes.

Immediately following Dr. Leopold's presentation, the staff discussed with him some of the implications of his concepts. Subsequently, two seminar sessions were devoted to examining the significance of crisis theory for the agency's casework practice. The three discussion periods are briefly summarized here.

The first question raised in the discussion of Dr. Leopold's presentation concerned the case illustration in which an illegitimate pregnancy was dealt with as a crisis. The questioner suggested that illegitimacy is not so much a personal crisis as it is a crisis for society. Dr. Leopold, however, expressed his opinion that a crisis is a subjective experience; it exists only when an individual *feels* it to be a crisis.

Another question raised was whether a maturational crisis is qualitatively different from a situational crisis. Dr. Leopold said he considered the term *situational crisis* a redundancy. A crisis always occurs within a comparatively short time span, he said, whether or not it is related to a defined stage of maturation. The term *situational crisis* is used to signify that a specific situation has created a temporary state of imbalance—for example, the mourning period that follows a death or the acute uncertainties in adolescent development. Such disturbances are very different from the disturbance of a child whose acting-out behavior has become an entrenched pattern and from the disturbance of a psychotic person who has retreated into psychosis as a primary way of life. In these instances, what may have started as a crisis has become an illness.

In some instances, one crisis quickly follows another, with the result that crisis becomes a pattern of life.

One of the points stressed in the discussion was that an emergency and a crisis are not identical. An emergency is a situational threat; it becomes a crisis when the person who is faced with the threat becomes anxious and begins to explore his capacity to do something about it. As a professional helper, the caseworker needs some knowledge of the client's history of coping with crises in order to decide how much the client can do for himself and how much he himself should intervene, as well as to determine the appropriate timing, level, and method of intervention. The point was made that a person can weather a crisis effectively without utilizing community resources; he may find new resources within himself, or members of his family may give him enough support to master it.

To identify a crisis as such, the worker has to assess its duration and its appropriateness as well as the emotional response of the client.

No one goes through life without experiencing critical situations that involve threats to security, to health, or to happiness. In a crisis the person's normal coping capacity cannot handle the threat. The worker must intervene at the point at which the threat is acute because the client who is experiencing a crisis responds with anxiety; he comes to the realization that he cannot cope with the threat, and he wants to do something about it, although he may not know what to do.

In answering a question about the way in which a crisis should be handled when the worker knows that emotional problems have preceded the crisis, Dr. Leopold suggested that an attempt be made to get as much information as possible quickly and to solve the crisis first, but also to find out what the crisis means in terms of the individual's recent history. Most important, the client should be helped to strengthen his own coping capacities. Such help is usually a short-term service. But after the immediate crisis has been dealt with, the worker can determine whether there is need for further help. A diagnosis must be made quickly, and the client-worker relationship must be reality-oriented. Both flexibility and good judgment on the part of the worker are requisites. The crisis approach to treatment cannot be used with a sociopath, since he does not permit himself to experience anxiety.

In discussing the level of entry into a crisis situation, Dr. Leopold stated that the client usually offers several clues, on the basis of which the worker must choose where and how to enter. He said that intervening helpfully in a marital crisis is particularly difficult.

Dr. Leopold recommends that a follow-up interview be scheduled no later than three months after termination of crisis-oriented treatment. In such an interview the client has an opportunity to discuss his handling of the crisis, thereby strengthening his ability to deal with future problems and reaffirming "his dignity as a human being."

Dr. Leopold was asked to give examples of primary intervention—preventing crises from occurring. He gave two: (1) intervention during the prenatal period to help the mother understand, accept, and deal with what is happening to her and the child during pregnancy and the child's birth, and (2) intervention by school personnel through identifying a troubled child—who often is a troublesome child—so that he can be offered help in the early stages of his disturbance.

Three cases were reported as illustrations of crisis intervention and discussed by the seminar participants. In each case, four questions were the focus of attention: Is there staff agreement that a crisis existed? What kind of crisis was it? What was the worker's role? Was the worker's intervention helpful?

THE COOKE CASE*

Mr. Cooke, aged 30 years, teacher
Mrs. Cooke, aged 21 years, part-time graduate student
Daughter, aged 10 months

On March 16, Mrs. C, the twenty-one-year-old married daughter of Mr. and Mrs. H, telephoned the agency. She was a part-time graduate student in sociology. She had discussed her problem, which related to her parents, with a faculty member, Dr. S, and he had suggested she seek counseling help. Upon contacting the agency, Mrs. C said she wanted help in deciding how to deal with her mother during the visit she and Mr. C were planning to make at the home of her parents during the Passover holidays. Mrs. C, who was an only child, said her father was mentally ill and her mother was planning to leave him. Mrs. C was perplexed about what attitude she should take and what she should say to her mother. She said she would like an appointment before making that out-of-town visit to her parents' home on March 26.

FIRST INTERVIEW: MARCH 25

Mrs. C kept her first office appointment alone, feeling that the problem was primarily hers—and it was necessary, she said, for her husband to stay with the baby.

Mrs. C was a small, compactly built young woman, somewhat plain in appearance. She was bright, articulate, and highly knowledgeable. Although she used sociological terminology freely and appropriately, her presentation of her problem and her evaluation of it were not highly intellectual. She asked for specific advice about how to behave during the visit she, her husband, and the baby were about to make to her parents' home.

I encouraged Mrs. C to help me understand why the prospective visit presented a problem for her. She explained that her father had been mentally ill for the past four years. He had been hospitalized for a period of time, during which he had had electroshock treatment and some psychotherapy. The shock treatment seemed to have had some temporary value, but, she reported, he seemed to have been able to "con" the psychiatrist into believing he had improved substantially and discharging him.

Mrs. C's father, who was in his fifties, had been a successful schoolteacher until recently when, because of his paranoid thinking, he had had considerable difficulty with the school principal and teachers and been dismissed. Mrs. C described her father as a brilliant man and a highly skilled teacher with great persuasive ability. She said his paranoid thinking was

* Submitted by Mrs. Edith Shapin.

related to a sense of injustice in society and a conviction that it was his responsibility to correct the world's ills. Mrs. C said she had been able to tolerate the symptoms of her father's mental illness until recently, when she had learned that her mother had become a part of his paranoid system and the target of his verbal abuse, denigration, and goading. Mrs. H had told Mrs. C that she was planning to leave Mr. H because she could no longer tolerate his repetitious talking and abuse. A psychiatrist with whom Mrs. H had had some continuing contact since her husband's hospitalization had recommended that she consider a separation from Mr. H "for her own welfare."

Mrs. H's discussion of her plans to take this step, after twenty-seven years of marriage, had accentuated Mrs. C's conflict about her parents; she felt she must decide to which one she owed primary loyalty. With full recognition of her pain in this feeling of conflict, I suggested that Mrs. C tell me something of her relationship with her parents before her father's illness and before she left home to go to college. Mrs. C began to cry; she was embarrassed by her inability to control her tears and said that she did not know why she was crying now because she was generally well controlled—that, for the most part, she avoided thinking about this highly charged situation by absorption in her studies and in the care of her child. I let her know I understood her tears, that she need not exert herself to control her feelings, and that I thought no less of her for having showed them.

Mrs. C remembered feeling resentful of her father's giving so much of himself to his students and so little to her. She remembered her feeling of rejection at a time when he had pushed her aside, telling her to ask her mother for what she wanted. She said she had alway been closer to her mother (also a schoolteacher) than to her father, but she could say little about her mother except that she had been warm and protective.

It began to seem that Mrs. C tended to endow her mother with qualities that she actually did not have. Mrs. C said her mother had given to her abundantly. She felt it was her responsibility to return what she had received in full measure; she felt that only she could offer her mother a haven in her time of need by rescuing her from the intolerable situation in which she found herself. I said I could understand her wanting to make some return to her mother; I asked her, however, whether she was placing herself in the role of rescuer or her mother had asked her to provide her a refuge. She acknowledged that her own feelings were the chief factor, saying that her mother has not specifically asked her for help.

In answer to my question, Mrs. C reported that she and her husband had discussed her problem fully and that he was ready to support her in whatever decision she should make. As had Dr. S, with whom Mrs. C had discussed her problem, I questioned the wisdom of her tentative plan to invite her mother to live with her and Mr. C. Pointing out Mrs. C's own conflicted feelings, I suggested that Mrs. H might also be ambivalent in the situation. Mrs. C expressed surprise and dismay at the realization that she had not been able to consider anyone's feelings except her own and that she might be controlled by a desire to exchange roles with her mother. Mrs. C began to appreciate the fact that her mother's feelings and attitudes and a history of relationship with Mr. H were crucial to her decision about marriage. Mrs. C then agreed to my proposal that she invite her mother to spend part of her summer vacation with her, in the hope that through such a time-limited experience both she and her husband and Mrs. H might arrive at a valid plan based on the needs of all of them.

I returned to the issue of Mrs. C's proposed visit to her parents for the Passover holidays. She explained that she had visited her parents regularly on holidays since she had left home six years earlier in an effort to find her own identity and to become independent. She said that the visits had been pleasant until her father's illness but had become increasingly painful as a result of his paranoid thinking. She said that she and Mr. C tried not to argue with her father but that their attempts to pacify him and steer him away from controversial topics seemed to enrage him and lead him to accuse them of being against him. Mrs. C was able to acknowledge her feeling of shame about her father's illness, and during the discussion of her attitude became aware that her need was rather to learn to cope with her feelings about her parents than to have someone tell her how to behave in their presence. It then occurred to Mrs. C to wonder why she had not thought of inviting her parents to visit her for the Passover holidays and to speculate that it was perhaps appropriate for her, as wife, mother, and homemaker, to begin to take on some of the extra responsibilities that are appropriate to these roles. She was reminded that when her parents had visited her, tensions had been less than when she had visited them. She said that the baby's presence tended to dilute the stress arising from close contact with her father, that he could become absorbed in playing with the child, with the result that his paranoid thinking diminished. She said he became much more involved with the baby than he had ever been with her. Suddenly Mrs. C realized that one of the reasons she had not thought of inviting her parents to visit her during the holidays was her sense of being obliged to include her mother-in-law in any such invitation. She said she did not like her husband's mother, whom she thought to be her intellectual inferior, and felt she had nothing in common with her. With some chagrin, Mrs. C acknowledged being an "intellectual snob" and avoiding situations that brought her in contact with her mother-in-law. She said she supposed she would have to find some way of coming to terms with her husband's mother, whom she then described as "a good soul."

At the end of the interview Mrs. C commented that although I had given her no "advice" about how to behave during her visit to her parents, she had received considerable help from the discussion, felt less trepidation about being in her father's presence, and had a new perspective on the entire situation. She agreed to come back to talk with me after the visit.

SECOND INTERVIEW: MARCH 30

Mrs. C came to the office by appointment. She expressed amazement that the visit with her parents had gone so well and that she had managed not to get involved in any controversy with her father. Even so, she was aware of considerable underlying tension in herself, reflected in unusual cranki-ness on the baby's part. She recalled that although she had talked with her father, she had not been able to face him directly, which had distressed her. She said that, busying himself with the baby, he had not been aware of her discomfort.

Mrs. C reported that her father had conducted the Seder beautifully and that his interpretation of the Haggadah had been magnificent. She described how he had related the Exodus to the present struggle of the Negro for civil rights and associated his interpretation with his paranoid thinking and desire to right all the world's wrongs. She admired her husband's behavior during the visit, because he had treated her father as a person worthy of respect, and it was Mr. C's behavior that made her feel ashamed of her own discomfort. There had been times when she had wanted to escape from her father's presence but had forced herself to sit with him; she could not help remembering the kind of man he had been—a person respected by his friends and colleagues and a person of status in the community. Now his former friends had dissociated themselves from him and found excuses not to see him when he sought them out at the board of education. She said that her father knew they thought him to be mentally ill and that he had asked her directly whether she also did. She had been unable to answer him, knowing that his disturbance was increasing progressively and feeling that she must prepare herself for his eventual institutionalization. I could see that she was cushioning herself against such an eventuality and suggested that doing so was a way of learning to face reality.

Mrs. C reported that her mother had decided against an immediate separation from Mr. H. She said her mother seemed to have found a way of coping with Mr. H's illness, at least temporarily, that she seemed to be able to walk away from him when the strain of hearing him talk became too great and even to "tune herself out" in his presence. Mrs. C appeared to have gained some understanding of her mother's allegiance to Mr. H and her current inability to separate from him after so many years of marriage. Mrs. C expressed a feeling of relief that a separation was not imminent, and she was responsive to my recognition of her relief and of her ambivalent feelings. She was able to say that her mother's decision had taken her "off the hook" for the time being.

With Mr. C's support, Mrs. C had been able to reach the decision that they would visit her parents less frequently. She said she had based her decision on the difficulty of traveling with a baby and on the difficulty for the baby of adjusting to the change in environment. Although acknowledging the reality of these difficulties, I reminded Mrs. C that her own feelings had played a large part in her decision and suggested that the child's reactions might well be a reflection of her own ambivalent and conflicted feelings.

During the interview Mrs. C was able to give credit to her father for stimulating her to develop her intellectual capacities: he had stimulated her interest in Hebraic learning and encouraged her to get a sound background in Hebrew and in the Talmud. He himself had been educated in a yeshiva, as a result of his father's desire that he be well educated in Hebrew. Though he had been born in the Midwest, his father had sent him and his brother, accompanied by their mother, to attend school in New York. For many years they had lived in economic deprivation, but he and his brother had succeeded in getting the education their father had planned for them.

As Mrs. C outlined her father's background, she arrived at a new perspective. She realized he had been deprived of his father at an early age and had many unmet dependency needs. She concluded that the seeds of his mental illness had probably been sown in his early childhood—and she seemed to be concerned about whether she herself was carrying the seeds of potential illness and perhaps passing them on to her child. When I mentioned my thoughts about her concern, she said she wondered how I knew what she was thinking. She began to cry. I reassured her with the comment that current knowledge about mental health indicates that mental illness is not inherited—and I asked her to tell me more about her concerns. She said she supposed her anxiety was "foolish." After I had acknowledged the reality of her feelings, we discussed her anxiety; she was able to see herself as separate from her father and to realize also that her child's father was not her father. Mrs. C then spoke about her husband's even disposition and his ability to keep her "on an even keel." She thinks they complement each other and has concluded that she is fortunate to be married to him.

Mrs. C said she had received a "tremendous" amount of help from her two interviews and that, for the time being at least, she needed no more. I acknowledged my recognition that the experience had not been easy for her. In response she stated that she was "not accustomed to get undressed in public" but that she had found her experience with me less harrowing than she had anticipated. She said she had never before been on "the other side of the desk" and, to her delight, had found that her sense of herself as a "healthy" person had not been threatened. She paid tribute to my capacity to understand her and to give of myself without becoming "subjectively involved." She said she wished she could learn how "to interview so skillfully"; indicating an awareness of her own difficulty in becoming involved in interpersonal relationships, she acknowledged having deliberately chosen to major in sociological research and to prepare to teach on the college level in order to protect herself.

Although I was aware that Mrs. C had problems on which we had not touched, I was ready to agree with her that she had taken as much help as she could at the time. Although Mrs. C wanted to make the termination final, I encouraged her to telephone me in a month to let me know how things were going with her, and she seemed to feel free to get in touch with me sooner if she felt the need to do so.

TERMINATION: APRIL 30

Mrs. C telephoned as previously arranged, in about a month. She reported that "things" were "on an even keel." She said that her father seemed to have reached a plateau in his illness and that her mother said she could continue to cope with the situation as it was. Mrs. C reported that her parents had visited her the previous week end and that nothing "extraordinary" had happened. She expressed admiration of her mother's reactions and said she hoped she could meet a similar crisis as well. Mrs. C then asked whether she might call me if she felt she needed further help.

38

At the outset of the discussion of the Cooke case, the question was raised whether this case actually presented an example of a crisis situation. Staff opinion was divided. Those who felt it was an illustration of a true crisis pointed to the stress under which Mrs. C had been placed: she was experiencing a conflict about loyalty toward her father as against loyalty toward her mother. She had tried to repress the conflict but had had to deal with it. The coping capacities she had used in the past had been inadequate for dealing with her current situation, and the anticipated visit to her parents had been experienced by her as a crisis.

What was the crisis for Mrs. C? At least part of it was her being faced with the imminent separation of her parents and the question with which she confronted herself—"With whom shall I side?" It was her perception of the event that created the crisis for her.

Some of the coping methods clients often use were mentioned. Some have no anxiety about their problems, see their difficulties as the responsibilities of others, and seem to cope through the use of projection. Others cope with problems by acting out rather than by handling them directly. A client's response to a crisis, and the extent of his panic under stress, are directly related to his emotional health. Mrs. C was judged to be, basically, an emotionally healthy woman. If she had not been so healthy, she could not have reached out for help and responded so quickly by changing her attitude toward both parents.

In discussing what differentiates the casework handling of a crisis from the casework handling of other situations, the counselor questioned what would have happened in the Cooke case if she had not intervened immediately in the way she did. It was agreed that it was more than likely that Mrs. C would have interfered in her parents' marriage and then been burdened by feelings of guilt about what she would have perceived as disloyalty to her father. Because the counselor realized that the precipitating factor in Mrs. C's crisis was her loyalty conflict, it was this conflict that was chosen as the focus of casework intervention. The event that set off the crisis was the projected visit to her parents' home. Mrs. C was helped to cope with the acute anxiety aroused by the prospect of the visit and to face the present reality, her father's illness and her mother's ability to bear his illness and stand by her husband.

The event that precipitates a crisis and the client's way of perceiving and experiencing it are interrelated; they are equally important to the determination of the means and level of intervention. Mrs. C's perception of mental illness and her fear of passing on mental illness to her child were part of her motivation in coming to the agency. It was mentioned that in the Chinese language there are two characters for crisis: one character means danger and the other means opportunity. Mrs. C perceived her crisis as a danger, but she also sought in it an opportunity for getting the professional help she needed.

In the public health field, crisis theory is concerned with primary and secondary intervention. Primary intervention represents an attempt to prevent a crisis from occurring, as, for example, through premarital counseling. Secondary intervention is illustrated by the counseling given a young married couple who, unprepared for marriage, come to an agency after several years of marriage for help with marital and child-rearing problems. The Cooke case is an example of secondary intervention.

Finally, a question was raised about the amount of information the worker had to have about Mrs. C in order to be of help to her. The worker did not need a detailed history to determine the amount and kind of help that was needed; the worker required only an understanding of Mrs. C's coping pattern in the past and sound judgment about the appropriateness of Mrs. C's expressed feelings. Mrs. C was well able to deal with reality, to establish sound relationships, and to function with reasonable autonomy. On the basis of that knowledge the counselor could determine the proper level of intervention: accordingly, Mrs. C was encouraged to face her situation and was helped to clarify her ideas about mental illness. In the process Mrs. C's confidence in both her own and her mother's strengths was increased.

THE HOFFMAN CASE*

Mr. Hoffman, aged 33 years, salesman
Mrs. Hoffman, aged 31 years, housewife
Daughter, aged 9 years
Son, aged 8 years
Son, aged 6 years
Son, aged 4 years

The contact was initiated by Mrs. H at a time when Mr. H was threatening to leave home after ten years of marriage because of his interest in another woman.

NATURE OF THE CONTACT

There have been six interviews with Mrs. H and five with Mr. H. The case is still active.

NATURE OF THE CRISIS

Mr. H. left home on the morning of Mrs. H's first interview, six days after her application. His feelings with respect to his wife and his paramour were confused, and he wanted a separation in order to think things through. The relationship with the paramour, who had been a close family friend, had existed for several months; she was planning to leave her husband immediately.

COURTSHIP AND MARRIAGE

Mr. H, who had been reared in another city, had met his wife when he had been visiting a relative in her home town. They had had several casual contacts followed by a two-year courtship. The parents of both had been opposed to their marrying because Mr. H was in the armed services and had not had a chance to establish himself. At least seven family conferences had been held in the course of the couple's effort to gain parental approval of the marriage; unable to win over their parents, the young people had eloped. They had gone first to live with Mrs. H's parents, been put out of the home, and then gone to live with Mr. H's parents. After considerable consultation between the two sets of parents, a religious ceremony had been arranged. Mrs. H had then joined her husband at the base at which he was stationed. Following his discharge three months later, Mr. and Mrs. H had moved into Mr. H's parents' small apartment. Several months had gone by before Mr. H had found employment and Mr. and Mrs. H had moved into an apartment of their own. Mr. H's father had not approved of the apartment

* Submitted by Mrs. Sadie Ginns.

and had offered to supplement the young people's income so that they could have more desirable quarters. Mr. H's employment had been irregular and his father had withdrawn financial support. Six years before the contact with the agency, when the H's had been in a critical financial state, they had accepted the invitation of Mrs. H's parents, who occupied a ranch house in the suburbs, to return to live with them. For some time before the application the relationship between Mr. H and his mother-in-law had been strained, as he fought her domination.

BACKGROUND

Both Mr. H and Mrs. H were only children of middle-class parents. Mrs. H had been overprotected by a domineering mother who set rigid standards, to which Mrs. H had usually conformed. Mr. H had been reared by his paternal grandmother because his parents were in business together. His father was harsh and demanding, considered himself the family decision-maker, and was usually entangled in the affairs of others. Life between father and son had always been a contest in which each spitefully attempted to demean the other verbally. Mr. H had been a disappointment to his father because he had not lived up to his father's expectation that he would follow a professional career. In his youth Mr. H had been conforming to the point of being called a sissy. When he had reached high school, there had been a complete reversal in his behavior; he had allied himself with questionable associates, truanted, and left school in the last term of his senior year because he was about to be expelled. Because everything seemed to be closing in on him, he had enlisted in the armed services.

PREVIOUS COPING PATTERNS

Parents on both sides continued to be dominating factors in the couple's life, and Mr. and Mrs. H's unresolved dependence on the parents was heightened at points of crisis. Mrs. H sought peace at any price. Although resentful of her mother's attitude, she meekly submitted to her will and let Mr. H assume full responsibility for any differences that occurred. Mr. H had frequently expressed a desire to move out of the home, but Mrs. H had not supported him because of her unreadiness to make the separation. The H children were trained and disciplined by their grandmother.

Mr. H was impulsive and was subject to uncontrollable rages, during which he was violent. At the age of fifteen, he had slashed a girl's wrist; and he had burned his wife with a cigarette. He had walked out on his family; he had broken off his relationship with his paramour and then renewed it.

AGENCY INTERVENTION

Mrs. H, a healthy, intelligent woman, was helped to look at the factors that had led to her current situation and to consider the choices available to her, as well as the risks involved in whatever course she might take. Facing her situation was the beginning of the acceptance of adult responsibility for Mrs. H, and she was able to use the crisis for her own growth. Moving ahead quickly, she saw her need to separate from her family and took immediate steps in that direction. Within two months a house had been pur-

42

chased and she had moved. She was given encouragement and support in her striving for independence, which involved firmness in facing up to her mother's opposition and her mother's position with respect to the children. Direct intervention in several areas was also undertaken: examining Mrs. H's finances in relation to moving; helping her define her role as a separated wife; and helping her determine her position in relation to her husband's paramour.

Throughout the two months of service, Mr. H continued to be very much a part of his family, visiting almost daily, spending week ends, and often calling his wife several times a day and reporting to her conversations with his paramour, whom he saw daily. He derived considerable satisfaction from the illicit relationship, but, at the same time, he was fond of his wife and devoted to the children. Operating on an immature level, he was confused, guilt-ridden, and full of inner turmoil. He had obsessive dreams and believed he would come to a violent death at an early age; he projected the image of a clown and tried to create the impression of strength and decisiveness, whereas, in reality, he was indecisive and greatly fearful of his aggressiveness and hostility. He was surprised by his wife's new-found strength and shocked by the amount of maturity she displayed. He was given help in seeing that his blame of his parents, his mother-in-law, and his wife was projection. He was also given help in coming to the realization that he must take responsibility for getting more self-understanding, and he was referred for psychiatric treatment, which had been suggested some years earlier by the family doctor and encouraged by Mrs. H.

PRESENT SITUATION

An initial appointment with a therapist has been scheduled for Mr. H. Mrs. H has gained a sense of freedom and confidence. Initially fearful of being on her own, she is now proud of the steps she has taken. She no longer feels lost and believes that she is well able to stand on her own feet no matter what decision her husband comes to with respect to his family. At the same time, separation from her mother is a steady, ongoing process, despite her mother's continued attempts to retain a hold over her.

Discussion of the Hoffman case was begun with a statement to the effect that the case presented a crisis in that Mr. H had walked out on his family. In addition, he showed symptoms of progressive mental illness. His acute panic had resulted from his inability to handle the crisis precipitated by the need to make a choice between his paramour and his wife, and he had not even begun to cope with it. Mr. H had displayed a pattern of disturbance for many years. Rebellion against authority figures had highlighted his history. His acting out seemed to be, in part, a way of getting attention.

Mrs. H had a peace-at-any-price relationship with her mother and needed greater autonomy. Her husband's leaving her was a test of her strength and her ability to stand on her own feet. The crisis had come to a head when Mr. H's paramour had decided to leave her husband for Mr. H's sake.

In this case the worker's intervention began in the second interview with Mr. H, in which she centered on his personal difficulties and needs. Mr. H was obviously anxious; as his anxiety was relieved, dynamic energy was released, which he could use to overcome the crisis. If the worker had attempted to convince Mr. H to return to his wife, the result would probably have been an even more severe crisis. Instead, the worker used Mr. H's readiness for help to refer him for psychiatric treatment, a step he had not been ready to consider earlier. Mr. H was enabled to disentangle himself from threatening relationships and turn his attention to his inner turmoil.

The worker encouraged Mrs. H to test her strength and loosen the tie to her mother that had impeded her growth. In the crisis presented for both Mr. and Mrs. H, the marriage could not have been made the focus of treatment; each partner had to be given individual help to become extricated from an untenable and threatening situation.

THE RASTOW CASE*

Mr. Rastow, aged 44 years, counterman in cafeteria
Mrs. Rastow, aged 43 years, housewife
Son, aged 14 years, student

The R family had been in a displaced persons camp and had been re-settled in the community served by the agency twelve years before the initial contact. At first Mr. and Mrs. R had been hostile, demanding, and difficult to work with. After a short period of time Mr. R had secured work, and the family had become self-supporting except for occasional temporary assistance given by the agency during the following two-year period and subsequently in emergencies. Mrs. R had been ill for a considerable length of time, and the family had accumulated debts in order to pay for her medical care.

JANUARY 16

Mr. R arrived fifteen minutes late for his appointment. He was dressed in an extremely untidy fashion. He had stopped work December 30 and returned to work on January 14. Since he needed money enough to buy food for the next three days, he was given a check for $10 but was reminded that the agency could not continue to help him financially. I talked with him about HIAS' helping him to become a citizen; he said that all his papers were in order but that he did not have time to be bothered with applying for citizenship. He said he had applied for unemployment compensation, however, and might be eligible to receive a check for $40.

Mr. R stated that his wife was mentally ill, suffered from colitis, and might have diabetes. He said she was bothered by everything and periodically depressed, that she went to sleep at 3 A.M. and awakened at noon. He reported that three years earlier she had awakened "shaking" and been told by a physician that she was in good physical health and merely nervous; that she had been examined recently by a psychiatrist who had given her pills; and that she went continually from one physician to another. From his reports it appeared that Mrs. R had had a hysterectomy. He stated that during the past two years he had paid medical bills amounting to $800, and still owed $120, and that because of Mrs. R's medical bills, he owed the government $180 in unpaid taxes. He said that he and Mrs. R had had hospital insurance for the past three years. He said also that they might be eligible for some kind of pension from the German government for health damages; he reported that Mrs. R should receive $1,400. It appeared

* Submitted by Dora Salkin.

that Mr. R was not giving all the facts, and I was not sure whether what he was saying was true or distorted.

Mr. R reported that his son, fourteen years of age, was not doing well in school, supposedly because of infected tonsils, but was being tutored in arithmetic.

Since Mr. R comes to the agency only in emergencies and has refused to make himself eligible for public assistance, I think it inadvisable for the agency to give him further financial assistance.

JANUARY 31

Case closed.

AUGUST 26

Mr. R came to the agency without appointment to request emergency financial aid. He looked worried and tired but was carefully shaved and neat in appearance. The financial problems he reported involved a debt to the Internal Revenue Service and a constable's notice for nonpayment of rent; he said he had quit his job a few days earlier because his employer had refused to lend him money. (The Internal Revenue Service had attached his whole pay of $60, and he had nothing to live on.)

Mr. R and I discussed the meaning of the pattern of his contact with the agency over the years, and he agreed that emergency aid had not solved his problems. He said he was ready to seek help from HIAS in beginning his application for citizenship, to apply for unemployment insurance benefits, and meanwhile to look for work.

Following discussion with my supervisor, I offered Mr. R the opportunity to meet with a counselor to consider his problems in a more basic way. He accepted the offer, with the expectation of hearing from the agency within a few days. No financial aid was given.

AUGUST 29 AND AUGUST 30

I saw Mr. R on both August 29 and August 30. I spoke with him about the implicit irresponsibility of some of his actions, such as his walking out on his job. But I also spoke of my awareness that he had been carrying an extraordinary burden for many years, contributed to by inadequate wages, his wife's illness, and his assumption of financial obligations, such as loans, that he actually could not meet. I suggested he needed help in facing his problems realistically. He admitted that leaving his job had been a mistake; when he had quit previously, he said, his employer had called him back immediately, but this time he had not, and a week had passed. Mr. R said he had applied for a position in a delicatessen and been told to return after Labor Day, when a decision would be made whether he could be employed. He can read English fairly well, has a little difficulty in reading script, but has no difficulty in doing arithmetic. He had already applied for unemployment insurance, and, if accepted, would receive $39 a week. The constable's notice for nonpayment of rent—now two months in arrears— remained in effect.

I talked with Mr. R about the possibility of his reapplying for his former job. I also encouraged him to join the union, and he admitted he had been handicapped by not having done so before. I also suggested to Mr. R that if he could not find a job, the agency's Business Counseling and Loan Department might help him start a small business of his own. Having presented all these possibilities, I offered temporary financial help amounting to $12 for food. Mr. R was disappointed at my not offering to pay his rent. He agreed to telephone the agency the day after Labor Day, to learn who his ongoing counselor would be. (Since evaluation of advisability of a business loan is involved, this case would also be referred to the agency's Business Committee.)

SEPTEMBER 4

Mr. and Mrs. R came to the office in response to an appointment letter I had addressed to both of them, though Mrs. R's lack of involvement in the past had made me doubt she would come. Mrs. R tried to take over the interview, and I had to direct questions specifically to Mr. R to prevent his being excluded. Both Mr. and Mrs. R were very concerned about a letter from the constable informing them they must vacate their apartment by the following day. The constable had not asked for the $140 that was due, but for possession of the premises. Both Mr. and Mrs. R were adamant in their unwillingness to look for other quarters, saying that it would be difficult to find another apartment and costly to move. They expressed the hope that they could work out some solution with the owner, if the constable could be appeased. I explained that the constable was acting with the approval of the landlord and renting agent and urged the idea that finding a new apartment would enable them to make a new start without their having to be concerned about overdue rent. My arguments made no impression.

I telephoned from another office and spoke to the constable. He agreed to allow Mr. and Mrs. R to retain the premises if one month's rent was paid immediately; he insisted, however, that a second month's rent must be paid by September 26. I hoped that Mr. R would be employed by that time.

Mr. R said he was sorry he had quarreled with his employer and left the job. I pointed out that he should have realized that a time would come, after he had quit repeatedly, at which his employer would not take him back. Mr. R said that he had telephoned his employer and asked for his job again, without success. I suggested that Mr. R might be successful if he apologized for his angry words and stressed his need for his job, with which idea he agreed.

Mr. R admitted that in the past he had had six notices from the constable for nonpayment of rent and attributed his difficulty to large expenditures for medical care for Mrs. R. Addressing myself to both, I pointed out that as long as Mrs. R continued to visit a private physician several times a week, they would never be out of debt. I suggested that Mrs. R ask her regular physician to transfer her to the clinic at the hospital, where she could continue to see him for a smaller fee and purchase medication at less cost. Mrs. R was reluctant at first to consider my suggestion but later agreed to talk about it with her physician and signed an authorization for him to release information to the agency.

I raised the issue of budgeting and money management and encouraged Mr. and Mrs. R to work with the agency on these matters when Mr. R should again secure employment.

I again raised the issue of securing citizenship and pointed out that if Mr. R did not do so, the agency could no longer offer help even on a temporary basis. Mr. R admitted that on several occasions he had gone to HIAS and initiated application for second papers and that he had never followed through. He agreed to do so, however, and while the R's were in the office, I telephoned HIAS and made an immediate appointment for Mr. R. I pointed out that once the R's became citizens they would have to seek help from the public welfare agency if they needed financial assistance. I set up a budget with Mr. and Mrs. R and gave them an allowance for one week.

Later in the day I spoke directly to the renting agent, who agreed to accept one month's rent to be paid by the agency.

SEPTEMBER 12

Mr. R telephoned. He reported that he had apologized to his employer, that the employer had agreed to attest that Mr. R was unemployed because of lack of work, and that he had filed an unemployment compensation claim. He said he had two appointments to be interviewed for jobs. Moreover, he reported that he had spoken to his landlady and that she had agreed not to take any action to dispossess him and his wife.

Discussion of the Rastow case began with the observation that the family had presented one crisis after another, that a state of crisis had thus become a part of its life style. For the R's, crisis was circular, and they were unable to break out of the cycle. Immediate intervention was therefore required, focused on the most recent crisis. Not all staff members agreed that the R situation presented a true crisis. Some saw Mr. R as a man for whom crises were more nearly a pattern of behavior than distinct occurrences at various points in time. Moreover, Mr. R seemed to have learned to live with this pattern with minimal anxiety.

The observation was made that the kind of situation presented by the R family can easily arouse a feeling of hopelessness in the worker, and it was pointed out that a great deal of work is involved in handling such a case, owing to the many environmental problems that have to be tackled. Question was raised about the nature of the intervention called for. Three factors were stressed: (1) the need to determine with whom the worker should deal primarily; (2) the need to set specific goals, both environmental

48

and psychological; and (3) the need to establish a structure geared both to solving environmental problems and to strengthening the client's coping capacity. The point was stressed that clients like Mr. R must be helped to see the connection between inner and outer problems.

In this case, the worker brought Mr. R's attention to his past failure to complete the necessary procedures for obtaining citizenship and pointed out the benefits he could derive from doing so. Under the pressure of his critical situation, Mr. R took an immediate step to follow through on this matter. He had needed someone to define and differentiate his problems, to set priorities, and to help him recognize what had happened in his life to get him into his present predicament. Moreover, he needed somebody to stand by him so that he would not again be overwhelmed by hopelessness and confusion.

2

CONFLICTING FORMAL AND INFORMAL ROLES IN NEWLY ACCULTURATED FAMILIES*

John P. Spiegel

Communication problems can be described within a number of different conceptual frameworks. In the course of studying disturbed interpersonal relations within families undergoing acculturation from an Old World set of cultural values to those of the urban United States, my colleagues and I have used the concept of social role to describe such problems.[1] Up to the present we have studied Italian-American, Irish-American, and Greek-American families, contrasting them with "Old American" families—all at working-class levels; but, because of time, I will present data only on Italian-Americans. Since, in our approach, so much of the burden of explanation of communicative behavior rests upon the social role concept, it may be well at the outset to define the way in which the concept of social role is to be used.

* Reprinted from *Disorders of Communication*, Vol. XLII, Research Publications, 1964, by permission of the Association for Research in Nervous and Mental Disease, New York, N. Y. The investigation has been supported by a grant from the National Institute of Mental Health. It is sponsored by the Laboratory of Social Relations, Harvard University, and the Children's Medical Center, Boston.

[1] John P. Spiegel, "The Resolution of Role Conflict within the Family," *Psychiatry*, Vol. XX, February 1957, pp. 1–16; Spiegel, "Interpersonal Influences within the Family," in *Group Processes*, Bertram Schaffner (ed.), Josiah Macy, Jr., Foundation, New York, 1956; Spiegel, "Some Cultural Aspects of Transference and Countertransference," in *Individual and Familial Dynamics*, Jules H. Masserman (ed.), Grune & Stratton, New York, 1959, pp. 160–82; and Spiegel and Norman W. Bell, "The Family of the Psychiatric Patient," in *American Handbook of Psychiatry*, Vol. I, Silvano Arieti (ed.), Basic Books, New York, 1959, pp. 114–49.

A social role can be defined as a goal-directed configuration of acts patterned in accordance with cultural value orientations for the position a person holds in a social group or situation. This definition takes account of the fact that roles are developed within social systems for some purpose or end of the social system: the role of the parent is to bring up children. The goal of a salesman is to sell; that of an educator is to educate. But the behaviors which are assembled within the role in the pursuit of its goals vary greatly from one culture to another. English, Jewish, Arabic, and Indian parents each behave differently toward their children and expect different behavior from them. For this reason, one cannot obtain an accurate description of any role without at the same time ascertaining the cultural values which pattern the acts included within the role.

Another important aspect of this definition of social roles is that it assumes that roles never exist in a vacuum, but always in a social group or situation. In other words, the communicative behavior to which the role refers always occurs between two or more people who may be defined as role partners. The behavior is then to be understood as occurring in role systems composed of the reciprocal, geared-in acts of the role partners. If the acts do not gear in with each other—if they do not fit—then there will be conflict in the role system or, as we usually say, between the role partners.

The purpose of this paper is to trace the origin and the fate of formal role conflicts appearing within nuclear families—that is, between the husband and wife and between parents and children. We have found that once formal role conflicts become firmly established in the family, they are likely to give rise to informal role conflicts which drain the conflict away from the formal role system in which they begin and work in such a way that the real origin of these conflicts is obscured. Subsequently, communications take place around the secondarily involved informal roles. Since these roles are not concerned with the real causes of conflict, such communications serve to increase rather than reduce tension.

In order to demonstrate how this process works, I must now set forth, in a rather abstract and brief way, two somewhat formidable classification systems. The first one is a sketch of the classification of cultural values which characterize the formal roles of the Italian-American families that we have been studying. These cultural values will be contrasted with those of the American middle-class family toward which the Italian-Americans are moving in the acculturation process.

The classification system which I will present is based upon the theory of variation in cultural value orientations which was developed by my colleague Florence R. Kluckhohn.[2] The theory states that value orientations are highly generalized solutions of common human problems. Second, the theory proposes that these solutions have an evaluative component, which means they serve as principles for making preferred selections between alter-

[2] Florence Rockwood Kluckhohn, "Family Diagnosis: Variations in the Basic Values of Family Systems," *Social Casework*, Vol. XXXIX, February–March 1958, pp. 63–72, and Kluckhohn and Fred L. Strodtbeck, *Variations in Value Orientations*, Row, Peterson and Co., Evanston, Illinois, 1961.

native courses of action; an existential component, which means that the value orientations help to define the nature of reality for those who hold the given values; and, finally, an affective component, which means that people not only prefer and believe in their own values but are also ready to bleed and die for them. For this reason, values, once formed, can be changed only with the greatest difficulty.

There are five common human problems whose solutions form the classification schema of the value orientations. There are three possible solutions for each of these problems, and the theory states that each of the three possible solutions exists in every culture, though with a different ranking in the order of preference. Because of the shortness of time, however, I shall present only the first, or dominantly preferred, solution for each of the categories, illustrating first by reference to the American middle-class family, then passing to the Italian-American family. The value orientations to be described for the Italian-Americans are those characteristic of the native peasant cultures in southern Italy.

The first common human problem is concerned with the *time* dimension. This breaks down into the natural division between Past, Present, and Future. The American middle-class family much prefers the Future for all sorts of choices and decisions. Prospective parents plan for their children's future before they are born, save for their old age, and are always watching the clock or inspecting their schedules and calendars to see what they will be doing next. They expect change and prefer anything new to anything old. Because they hate to be old-fashioned or out-of-date, they often overestimate their capacity to face the need for change when it comes. The Italians, on the other hand, prefer the Present over the Past or Future. They live in an extended present in which the future is scarcely differentiated from the past. They believe that things have always been the same and always will be. Accordingly, if change should come, it is usually for the worse. Time is demarcated for them not by the accusing clock or calendar, but by leisurely cycles of seasons, religious feasts, national holidays, anniversaries, and ceremonial occasions of all kinds.

The second value orientation category is concerned with *relationships within groups* and is therefore called the relational category. The three possible solutions for this common human problem are the Lineal, the Collateral, and the Individualistic. Americans prefer the Individualistic solution. Parents train their children from an early age to stand on their own two feet, to control themselves, and to make their own decisions. Families live in small groups of parents and children and think nothing of pulling up roots and moving off to another part of the country, leaving their relatives behind. The Italians, in contrast, prefer the Collateral solution. They prefer to live in big families in close proximity to relatives, and if anyone has to go away, it is a tragedy for all concerned. Children are trained to be dependent upon their elders and on each other. If anyone makes an independent decision, he is looked on as disloyal or uncaring.

The third category is concerned with the preferred mode of *activity*. The solutions here are Doing, Being, and Being in Becoming. The Doing solution is preferred by Americans, who are always interested in each other's achievements. Parents train children to compete for success—in school, in sports, and in social life; and they anxiously review their own records as parents, comparing themselves in this way, as in every other, with their friends and enemies. Italians prefer the Being solution. Success and achievements are not nearly so important as expressing one's moods, feelings, and desires. Children are impatiently scolded or punished one minute and effusively given affection the next. What is always expected is spontaneity of feeling. To the Italian, accordingly, self-control for the sake of achievement, as it is practiced by Americans, looks hypocritical and exploitive.

The fourth category involves the *relationship between man and nature*. The solutions are Subjugation to Nature, Harmony with Nature, and Mastery over Nature. The last is the dominant preference of American middle-class families. Man is expected to triumph in any contest with nature, in accordance with the optimistic confidence in the power of science and technology. Disease and outer space are rapidly yielding to research; weather control is just around the corner; and we may yet learn how to avoid wars and other severe catastrophes. For any problem encountered by the family, there is always an expert who can be found in the Yellow Pages. In contrast, the Italian families prefer the Subjugation to Nature solution. This is, of course, in accordance with their religious ideology. Man is considered weak and helpless, and his only hope lies in recognizing this fact. He is dependent upon the Deity and the saints and is also the prey of malevolent powers, such as the evil eye, and magical curses, spells, and incantations. The most common reaction we heard from the Italian-American faced with a severe problem was the fatalistic expression: "What can I do?" This means that it is better to recognize one's weakness than to have false pride and unrealistic hopes.

The last value category is concerned with the *basic nature of man* in terms of Good and Evil. The concepts within this category are that man is born Evil though he is nevertheless perfectible; that man is born either Neutral or a mixture of Good and Evil; and that man is born Good but is nevertheless corruptible. The Italians believe that man is a mixture of Good and Evil. In a family with many children one or two may turn out to be mainly Good—and these will be expected to become priests or nuns—and one or two will turn out mainly Evil—and these will be black sheep. The remainder will be real mixtures of both. Such children are expected to be little devils one minute and little angels the next, thus calling forth the quick spontaneous response of anger or love in the parent. Americans, on the contrary, believe that children are born neither Good nor Evil but Neutral. How they turn out depends upon the nature of the parents' relation with the child. If the child misbehaves, the parents reason with him, and if misbehavior becomes serious, the child is regarded as maladjusted and the parents hold themselves responsible for the emotional problems in the child. Italian parents, on the other hand, would regard such a problem as revealing the innately Evil nature of the child, for which they could not possibly be held responsible.

This brief sketch of the two value orientation profiles reveals the extent of the cultural gap that confronts Italian families when they arrive in this country. It is true that some families arrive with values that have already begun to shift in the direction of the American pattern. Even so, it takes a long time before the process of acculturation makes much of a change in the Italian's value system. As the shift takes place, however, the spouses in these families often find themselves in conflict with each other because the shift to the American value orientation pattern has been unequal. Some of the American values have been partly adopted while the old, native patterns have not been wholly relinquished. This produces an internal ambiguity or malintegration of values within the individual which is not at all rare in a melting-pot country such as ours is. One often hears the value ambiguity communicated in the expression: "Do as I say, not as I do!" At any rate, because formal roles are patterned by the value orientations, the relationship between the spouses becomes strained and the strain then filters into other role systems. But, before this phenomenon can be described, it is necessary to present the second set of categories which I mentioned previously—that is, a general classification of social roles.

Social roles can be divided into three major categories: formal, informal, and fictive. Formal roles can be characterized in several different ways. They include the major activities which every society needs to regulate in order to survive. Some, like age and sex roles, concern straight biological functions and are universally ascribed to every member of the society—that is, not for one moment can anyone safely step out of the behavior expected for his age or sex. Some, like domestic or family roles, are almost as universally and inevitably ascribed since everyone is born into a family and most people create new ones. Still others, like occupational, religious, and recreational roles, while more episodic—that is, one does not need to occupy all of them all the time—are nevertheless strictly patterned and required for most people.

Informal roles, on the other hand, are much more occasional and at the choice of the individual than are formal roles. Some have to do with transitional occasions—that is, with getting out of one situation and into another. The sick role, for example, is such a transitional role, which the ill person may or may not agree to take. By the same token, some people, usually called malingerers, may take the sick role when they are not actually ill. At any rate, the sick role is informally patterned in every society in order to get the ill person back into a state of health. Visitors, guests, and travelers are also examples of transitional roles. Another group of informal roles is character roles. These include heroes and villains, liars and cheats, exhibitionists and voyeurs, sadists and masochists. Such behaviors are usually thought of as traits of character, but a moment's reflection reveals that the given behavior cannot take place without the reciprocal behavior of a role partner. Every hero must have his admirers, every exhibitionist must locate his voyeur, just as every masochist needs to find his sadist in order to enjoy his role in life. But such roles are not required of anyone by the social system. They may be adopted by one person or assigned to another, such as when we assign the role of a fool to someone we do not like. Such adoptions and assignments are, then, parts of the informal workings of social groups.

The third category, fictive roles, includes roles which are not pragmatically related to the ongoing work of any social system or group but which serve the interests of imagination or play. For the most part, they are occupied quite deliberately on the basis of pretense, such as when a girl plays the role of mother to her doll or a boy plays cops and robbers. All fictive roles make room for fantasy behavior in everyday life and thus serve the purpose—for adults as well as children—of relief from the stress and strain of reality. Every society sanctions such roles provided they are accompanied by a communication that says: This is not serious; this is in jest or play. When fictive or fantasy roles are taken without this accompanying signal, that is, in earnest, then we say that the behavior of the person who shows such behavior and the group which accepts such behavior is pathological. I am referring to the difference between the person who pretends to be the prophet Elijah, for the sake of amusement or satire, and the person who says he *is* the prophet Elijah and his followers accept this claim—a situation that approximately fits the current social arrangements of the Black Muslim sect.

I should now like to illustrate the observation I made at the beginning of this presentation: that formal role conflicts between the parents of families undergoing acculturation, based on incompatibility of value orientations, are likely to be deflected into informal roles where they become almost insoluble, without outside help. The reason for the pathological fixation of the conflict in the informal role systems is that none of the family members is aware of the nature of the communication problem. They do not realize that they are involved in an incompatibility of values, and they do not recognize that they have displaced their disagreements into the area of informal roles—or, if they realize it, they have too much anxiety about bringing the disagreement out into the open in the areas in which it really lies.

I should like to illustrate this process by telling you about a second-generation Italian-American family that we shall call the Tondi family. At the time we began our investigation, Mr. T was thirty-seven years old, Mrs. T was thirty-five, and they had two children, Kenneth, nine years old, and Albert, nicknamed Buddy, who was seven. The family had been referred to the outpatient psychiatric clinic of the Children's Medical Center because of Buddy, who suffered from severe constipation of functional origin. In addition he was a stutterer. During the diagnostic work-up of the family, it became clear that Kenny, the older brother, also had symptoms. He also was a stutterer; he suffered from a school phobia and he had various eating problems. It was Mr. T who had brought Buddy to the hospital, thus initiating the diagnostic process. It was from Mrs. T that we learned, with some reluctance on her part, of Kenny's disturbances. This was obviously an unusual arrangement since it is ordinarily the mother who brings a child to a clinic and who makes the complaints about the child. This behavior, therefore, set the stage for our inquiry into the nature of the communication process in the family: Why was it the father who assigned the sick role to Buddy rather than the mother, and why did he not assign the sick role to Kenny, who was equally, if not more, disturbed?

This family was accepted for study. Diagnostic and therapeutic interviews were held with the parents and with both children at the clinic and in the home. As our investigation proceeded, we discovered a number of other disturbances in the relation between formal and informal roles in the family. It turned out that Mrs. T's definition of the nature of Buddy's bowel dysfunction was ambiguous and somewhat bizarre. She saw the constipation partly as a physiological dysfunction and partly as willful disobedience. For example, she believed that if Buddy would only agree to her giving him an enema every other day, his constipation would be controlled. On his part, Buddy was extremely frightened by the enemas and terrified of having a bowel movement, even though he knew he experienced pain if he withheld his stool. Accordingly, he frequently lied to his mother, saying he had had a movement when he actually had not. Mrs. T was able to recognize the lie at the point at which he was obviously in pain. Realizing what was coming, Buddy would then attempt to hide. This was then defined by his mother as disobedience. She would become anxious about the damage he was doing himself and angry about his disobedience and would end up chasing him about the house in order to give him an enema, thus creating a scene which was frightening to both children. When Buddy refused to take the sick role as his mother defined it, she perceived this as evil and assigned Buddy the role of rascal and troublemaker. In return, Buddy saw himself in the role of victim of his mother's ministrations.

Buddy's role as rascal was generalized to other occasions. For example, Buddy, though younger, was strong and well-built, while Kenny was slender and poorly co-ordinated. When Buddy tried to protect Kenny in neighborhood fights, Mrs. T would accuse Buddy of having started the fight in order to cause trouble. Buddy was in general treated by the parents as the older and stronger, while Kenny was given the role of the younger and weaker son. This reversal of age roles fit in with the defenses of the children, for reasons which I cannot go into because of lack of space.

Of the many similar disturbances in informal roles, I shall mention just one more. Whenever Mrs. T visited her relatives, she took Kenny with her, leaving Buddy at home. When Mr. T visited his relatives, he took Buddy along, leaving Kenny at home. In general, Kenny was mother's boy and Buddy was father's boy.

Now we must ask: What do these distortions of the informal roles signify? What did they mean to the parents? How were they brought about? To answer this we must look at the history of the parents' involvement in their formal roles. Here, again, I can present only a few of the many aspects of this history.

Mrs. T's parents had been born in Italy, and her mother considered herself socially superior to her father, as well as to most of the other Italian-American families in the neighborhood. As an adolescent, Mrs. T was not considered attractive, and later she had few boy friends. Mr. T was the only man who asked her to marry him. Her family, however, considered his family socially inferior and discouraged the relationship. Since Mrs. T's relational orientations, like her family's, were collateral, she followed their wishes. When, after several years, no other prospect appeared and Mr. T refused to be discouraged, they finally gave in and sanctioned the marriage on the ground that she was not getting any younger.

Mr. T was the youngest of many children of native-born Italian parents. His father had died when he was a small child, and his mother had managed to support the family, with the aid of the older siblings. Because of the hard economic struggle, because of his native intelligence, and because his older siblings had broken a path for him, Mr. T had learned some of the middle-class American value orientations. He was able to plan for the future and to work for achievement. He was an airplane mechanic with good opportunities for advancement. But his family actually was somewhat lower on the socioeconomic scale than his wife's, though not as much as her family claimed. To him, the social difference meant that his wife could help him on the road to success in American terms, and therefore the marriage represented an achievement, while to his wife and her family it represented a failure.

After several years of marriage, Mrs. T continued to believe herself more American than her husband and superior to him. Accordingly, she could see little to value in him. Actually, she was much closer to Italian values, as was shown in the persistence of her collateral ties to her own family and in the innately Good and Evil, Being, and Subjugation to Nature values which she showed toward her children.

Because of her frequently derogatory attitude toward him, Mr. T gradually began to respond with a bitterness and resentment which he was unable to express and of which he was largely unaware. He warded off these feelings by saying that his wife was irritable and nervous because of the claims made on her by her family. Thus his overt attitude toward his wife was calm and reasonable, if long-suffering.

Covertly, however, and unconsciously, he found a way to express his resentment and to communicate to his wife his criticism of her value orientations. Buddy, the younger son, had always been stronger than his sickly older brother. By appropriating Buddy as his child, Mr. T was trying to show his wife how an American child—and an American male, as well—should be treated. By turning Kenny over to his wife, he was saying in effect: Kenny is your problem, the result of your inadequate and incompetent behavior as a wife and mother. Mrs. T, implicitly understanding this message, then attempted to retaliate by attacking Buddy's independence and assertiveness. Thus she was unwittingly maintaining the Collateral, Present, and Being values of the Italian culture, while also covertly retaliating against her husband's covert criticism by attacking his effigy, Buddy. It was this covert and displaced conflict which Mr. T tried to bring to an end by the typical American expedient of bringing the problem to an appropriate expert.

It is probably unnecessary to point out the pathological consequences for the children of becoming involved in such a displaced conflict. It is probably also unnecessary to say that there are many other aspects of such unconscious role conflicts besides the matter of the communication of cul-

60

tural values. Nor is it possible, here, to demonstrate how these role conflicts were loosened by psychotherapy with the family.[3] My purpose in this presentation has been merely to emphasize the merit of using the concepts of value orientations, social role, and unconscious communications to sort out the complicated data of family interactions.

In the seminar session following Dr. Spiegel's presentation, the group examined the application of his outline of value orientation categories to the client group the agency serves. The vast majority of the clients were thought to hold American middle-class cultural values and, in addition, certain values rooted in the Jewish tradition. The mixture of these two value systems and the relative predominance of one system over the other vary from family to family and from individual to individual.

TIME

American middle-class families are future-oriented. Buying on the instalment plan, for example, means having what is wanted in the present; but it also means trusting that the future is predictable and can offer continued security. An even clearer reflection of the dominance of a future-oriented attitude is the emphasis on youth and on long years of education: tomorrow, the younger generation will inherit the world. In this regard, there is no difference between the middle-class American orientation and the Jewish orientation.

Another expression of American society's orientation to the future is the widespread rejection of the aged, who have little future left to them. In its rejection of the aged, the younger generation is expressing its fear of its own ultimate future—sickness, unproductivity, and death. Those Jewish families that have retained Old World values still have a feeling of respect for the aged, a respect that sometimes borders on veneration.

RELATIONSHIPS WITHIN GROUPS

While the American culture, in general, stresses an Individualistic solution and separation from kinship ties, the Jewish community still maintains a system of Lineal and Collateral kinship ties, and family relationships are primary. This value orientation is, however, in a state of flux. As it shifts

[3] See also Ezra F. Vogel and Norman W. Bell, "The Emotionally Disturbed Child as a Family Scapegoat," *Psychoanalysis and the Psychoanalytic Review*, Vol. XLVII, Summer 1960, pp. 21–42; Bell and Vogel (eds.), *A Modern Introduction to the Family* (rev. ed.), The Free Press, New York, 1960; Bell, Albert Trieschman, and Vogel, "A Sociocultural Analysis of the Resistances of Working-Class Fathers Treated in a Child Psychiatric Clinic," *American Journal of Orthopsychiatry*, Vol. XXXI, April 1961, pp. 388–405; and Bell, "Extended Family Relations of Disturbed and Well Families," *Family Process*, Vol. I, September 1962, pp. 175–93.

from one generation to the next, it becomes an area for conflict between parents and children as well as between siblings.

ACTIVITY

American culture is geared to Doing, emphasizing action and results. In general, the Jewish community shares this value. But there is a segment of the Jewish community whose value is that of Being in Becoming. Persons who give primacy to this solution have an intense interest in education, not as a means to status and economic gain, but as an end in itself.

THE RELATIONSHIP BETWEEN MAN AND NATURE

Most Americans see themselves as masters over nature, and such an attitude may be reinforced as science develops further. Jews feel that they are in Harmony with Nature as long as they believe in God as the Creator. As the number of European-Jewish immigrants decreases, the American Jewish community is moving toward a Mastery over Nature orientation.

THE BASIC NATURE OF MAN

Contrary to Dr. Spiegel, the staff was of the opinion that American society tends to hold that children are born Good but are corruptible. It was suggested that the Jewish community holds the view that a child is born with a mixture of Good and Evil and is perfectible.

CONCLUSION

Differences of opinion among staff members, who themselves have widely different backgrounds, showed how complicated it is to trace cultural patterns in a melting-pot society. At the same time, there was general agreement that value differences have important implications for casework practice, inasmuch as a client's behavior can be understood only if it is viewed, in part, as an expression of his conscious and unconscious values.

62

THE BOLIN CASE*

Mr. B, aged 36 years, businessman
Mrs. B, aged 33 years, housewife
Son, aged 9 years
Son, aged 6 years
Son, aged 3 years

Mr. B telephoned identifying a marital problem, and a screening interview was scheduled for several days later. At that time Mr. B said he felt foolish in actually coming to the agency and suggested that his problem was not so bad after all. In the early part of the interview he defined his concern exclusively in terms of constant quarreling with Mrs. B. But toward the end of the interview he said that the primary problem was Mrs. B's reluctance to have sexual intercourse as frequently as he wanted it.

Mr. B explained that his father's death two weeks previously had led him to realize that life was short and to conclude that he wanted a more satisfactory relationship with his wife.

AGENCY EXPERIENCE

Mr. B and Mrs. B were seen separately for a total of eleven interviews each. They were seen jointly on fourteen occasions. At first Mrs. B was reluctant to involve herself. Even after doing so, she was able to voice her ambivalence about risking herself in treatment. As she began to experience positive changes, however, she showed an increased desire to continue in treatment. Ironically, Mr. B, who had been the more motivated in the beginning, seemed to want to end prematurely, saying that "everything" was "just fine." It is more than likely that his readiness to discontinue was related to Mrs. B's own change. For the most part, the B's made good use of the agency's service. The gains they achieved in their own relationship seemed to be directly connected with Mr. B's family of origin, and, perhaps in less measure, with Mrs. B's.

BACKGROUND: MARITAL

When both were in their teens, Mr. B, having gotten Mrs. B's telephone number from a relative, had called her and made a blind date with her. He had not found her especially appealing and, over a period of more than a year, had made dates with her only twice. They had met again at a surprise "freedom party" given for Mr. B on his twenty-first birthday. Noticing that her shyness and timidity had disappeared and feeling that she was more mature, he had been more attracted to her. They had not begun dating

* Submitted by Hugh Rosen.

regularly at once, but eventually did date regularly. Mr. B had found Mrs. B increasingly more attractive, and they had fallen in love.

The B's had been married when Mr. B was twenty-two and Mrs. B was nineteen. They had lived with Mrs. B's mother, her second husband, and her younger brother. The first years of their marriage had been "pretty rough." Mr. B had frequently found Mrs. B too tired for sexual intercourse, which she seemed to enjoy not at all at the beginning of their marriage and only minimally later. Mr. B had been disappointed; married life had not turned out to be what he had expected. Refused intercourse more times than he was "allowed," Mr. B had frequently felt that he would like to run around with other women but had never done so. Quarreling had begun fairly early in the marriage and continued throughout. After living with Mrs. B's mother and stepfather for two years, the B's had made independent living arrangements. At that time Mrs. B's mother had separated from her second husband and gone to live with the B's, along with Mrs. B's younger brother. When the B's first child had been born, Mrs. B's mother had taken an apartment of her own. The brother was in the Army.

It is noteworthy that Mrs. B said that Mr. B seemed to feel that his masculinity was compromised when he expressed tender feelings for her— when he said something of a tender nature to her, he always ended by making a joke of it. Mrs. B said she was gratified that Mr. B had come to the agency, thinking he would feel free to discuss his feelings with the worker and be helped to think differently.

BACKGROUND: MR. B

Both of Mr. B's parents had been born in the United States. He felt they had gotten along very well with one another. He referred to his father as being the boss and described him as a fearsome person. The children and Mr. B's mother had all been afraid of him, but, in Mr. B's opinion, he had been an intelligent man and a good father. Mr. B's early years had been spent in poor economic circumstances. A few years earlier Mr. B's father had entered Mr. B's scrap metal business; the association had been a disillusioning experience for Mr. B because it had shattered his image of his father as a good businessman.

Mr. B believed that he had always been his mother's favorite child and for this reason had always tried to live up to her expectations; he has always been "a good son." Mr. B has generally gotten along fairly well with his siblings, two younger sisters and a younger brother, though he feels that his sister Marion is somewhat aggressive. He feels that she and his mother have formed an alliance against Mrs. B and begun to "gang up" on her. Because of this he no longer feels that his mother is "the greatest."

BACKGROUND: MRS. B

Mrs. B had been an only child until she was six years of age, when her brother had been born. She had been sickly as a child; she had vague recollections of having been treated for a "club foot," and she had a history of digestive troubles. She had been close to her parents and a shy child. She had idolized her father and always expected to marry someone like him;

Mr. B had reminded her of her father when she had met him. After her father had died, when she was only sixteen, Mrs. B had developed colitis, and later she developed an ulcer.

Mrs. B had cared for her brother and did not remember ever having been jealous of him. He had been mischievous, and she had frequently intervened on his behalf. Her brother had begun to stutter at some point in his childhood, just when, Mrs. B was uncertain; she thought it might have been after their father's death, the cause of which Mrs. B was also uncertain about, although she thought it might have been either a heart or a kidney ailment.

Mrs. B's mother had been married three times. Both of her last two husbands had turned out to be alcoholics. Mrs. B's paternal grandfather also had been an alcoholic.

The relationship between Mrs. B's parents had been a good one, as she saw it. She herself had felt she could tell her mother about her problems, but the tendency in the family had been to avoid discussing problems with the mother for fear of worrying her. At the time of coming to the agency, Mrs. B said she felt free to argue openly with her own mother, though not with members of her husband's family. Mrs. B's mother had been "a doting mother" before the death of Mrs. B's father, but afterward had participated in a reversal of roles, as Mrs. B began to mother her.

NOTE: The material which follows represents selected excerpts from some of the interviews held with the B's. In most instances the complete recording of any one interview does not appear here.

FIRST JOINT INTERVIEW WITH MR. AND MRS. B

Somewhat unexpectedly, Mrs. B began the first joint interview by introducing the subject of Mr. B's masculinity. She said quite openly, as she had said earlier in an individual interview, that she felt Mr. B was uncomfortable in his masculinity and particularly in expressing tender feelings to her. Mr. B seemed puzzled and maintained that he did not know what Mrs. B was talking about. He attempted to interpret what she had said, however; he thought she was suggesting that he felt inferior and therefore had to make attempts to appear masculine. We pursued the subject together, and for the most part I let Mr. and Mrs. B talk to one another, which they seemed to do readily. Ultimately Mr. B said there might be some truth in what Mrs. B was saying and he felt he should give it some serious thought. I suggested that we might well examine the matter in future interviews.

Mr. B then took advantage of the situation by saying that he had recently become increasingly disturbed by the fact that Mrs. B was receiving more and more attention from other men. Several men had recently slapped Mrs. B on the buttocks and one man had kissed her on the shoulders. Mr. B thought many couples became "wild." He did not feel that Mrs. B purposely attracted the attention of other men; then, having a second thought, he began to speculate that she might actually be doing so. He thought Mrs. B was sexually appealing, and he wanted her to be appealing to other men. He added, however, that he would prefer Mrs. B to dress in a less sexually appealing way if it was her manner of dressing that was prompting men to make advances to her. Mrs. B denied that she was especially appealing to other men and also denied that she was unusually pretty. Mr. B insisted emphatically that she was very pretty and certainly should know that she was.

FOURTH INTERVIEW WITH MR. B

Mr. B opened the interview by complaining about Mrs. B's slowness, as he had frequently in earlier interviews. He said he often did not want to go out with her because she spent so much time dressing that they must then rush to be on time. He feels it is "a job just to get her moving." Frequently at the end of a movie Mrs. B remains seated, and it seems to Mr. B that she simply will not make the effort to get up and walk out. Mr. B then said that Mrs. B always seemed tired. Next, however, he said that when they went to weddings she never seemed to be tired and he had to prod her to leave. I said it was not clear to me what Mr. B was actually complaining about in this instance. He replied that, in reality, in such instances, Mrs. B was resisting a return to the routine of home life, including sex.

Every Sunday morning Mr. B gets up early and prepares breakfast for the children; he takes great pleasure in doing so but at the same time is annoyed that Mrs. B does not arise until eleven o'clock on Sundays. She, in turn, is angry at him for getting up early and preparing breakfast. Mr. B said that Sundays were "dangerous," meaning that he and Mrs. B are more prone to quarrel on Sundays than on other days.

FOURTH INTERVIEW WITH MRS. B

Discussing parental role, Mrs. B said she did not feel the children respected Mr. B as their father. She is disturbed by feeling this to be so. She respected her father and thinks that feelings such as hers are appropriate. Mr. B is not firm enough (manly enough?) with the children. She particularly resents his relying on her to discipline them; though she supports any assertion of authority on his part, he often undermines her authority with the children.

Mrs. B said that she felt "henpecked"—and I pointed out that her observation reinforced my impression that Mr. and Mrs. B were confused about their roles. Mrs. B added that Mr. B often accused her of not having a sense of humor and that she felt his accusation was unjust, because his "jokes" were usually barbed. He denies this. As we discussed the matter further, I said that Mr. B might well be expressing negative feelings in the form of a joke. I reminded Mrs. B of her previous statement that Mr. B seemed compelled to conteract any expression of positive feeling by some negative statement. Mrs. B remarked that Mr. B often slapped her "on the rear" when he said something positive to her—and she feels that his behavior is more hostile than playful.

A somewhat lengthy discussion followed about the B's sexual behavior and Mrs. B's attitudes regarding it. Mrs. B was active in trying to understand the sexual relationship more fully—and I strove to lead her to recognize that it was not an isolated matter, but an expression of their over-all relationship. Within this framework the problem was explored; Mrs. B

66

came to the conclusion that she used sex to punish Mr. B, to express the anger that she did not express directly. Recollecting some of her past, Mrs. B said that when she had married, her mother had given her only one piece of advice—never to refuse her husband sexual intercourse. At the time, Mrs. B was shocked to learn that some women do refuse to have intercourse with their husbands; she had been of the opinion that all wives love their husbands and so naturally always want to accommodate them. She said that she could not possibly have intercourse with a stranger upon first meeting, that she would have to have time to develop a favorable relationship. Immediately afterward she said, "Sometimes I feel as if my husband is a stranger." I suggested that she seemed to be saying that she needed to develop a generally satisfying relationship with her husband before she could enjoy their sexual relationship.

FIFTH INTERVIEW WITH MR. B

In discussing the children, Mr. B said he was content with them and felt he had a good relationship with each one. He complained that Mrs. B frequently asked him to discipline them when he saw no need to do so, and he complained further that, under such circumstances, Mrs. B should at least point out to him what the children were doing that required him to discipline them.

In examining the marital relationship, Mr. B was able to discover and reveal a fundamental and significant pattern. When he had first met Mrs. B he had been "just coming out of his shell," beginning to feel self-confident and adequate. Mrs. B had been shy and quiet; Mr. B had felt she needed and depended upon him, and this feeling had bolstered his ego further. He felt there had been a complete reversal in the relationship—and that he would not choose to marry Mrs. B under the current circumstances. He referred to her being outgoing and confident and specifically mentioned her recognition of her attractiveness. I pointed out that this development in Mrs. B had been largely the result of Mr. B's support of her and his own frequent reminders to her of her assets. He thought this to be an ironic truth in that he currently felt inadequate and thought Mrs. B could "get a better man." He believes he is aggressive and dynamic at work; when he comes home in the evenings, however, he feels like a little boy and would like to be able to lay his head in her lap. But Mrs. B is no longer affectionate or responsive to such a mood.

SECOND JOINT INTERVIEW

The B's arrived thirty minutes late. Although Mr. B had not been able to leave his office as early as he had hoped, he had gone home and shaved and changed his clothes before coming to the agency. He was quite upset about being late, particularly because he had repeatedly complained to me about Mrs. B's lateness. A discussion followed of the differences in Mr. and Mrs. B's attitudes toward time. Mr. B became aware of his attitude toward it: "It's true, I can never relax," he said. I made use of his comment to point out to Mrs. B that Mr. B's criticism of her "slowness" was not so much a personal criticism as it was an expression of his problem, mentioning that he was being as harsh with himself for being late as he had ever been with her.

Toward the close of the interview we were discussing Mr. B's father as a provider; he said that in recent years he had realized that his father had been a better provider than his mother had led the children to believe. When I asked Mrs. B how she felt about her husband as a provider, she said enthusiastically that she had no worry at all about being provided for, that she had full confidence that Mr. B could always earn a good living. He seemed very pleased; he asked her several questions directly about his working ability, all of which she answered in a way that affirmed her confidence in him. Mr. B said that he too felt he was a good provider, had confidence in his ability to earn a living, and, lastly, felt he had something to work for. When I asked what that "something" was, he said, "My wife and children." I said I thought we had reached a good place to end the interview, unless Mrs. B wanted to add something. She said she was quite content to stop where we were. Nevertheless, she related, jokingly, an anecdote on the way out: She and Mr. B had gone to a restaurant for dinner after the last interview, and the waitress, upon learning that they were married and had three children, had asked how they managed to get along so well; Mr. B had replied, "By gin and tonics and counseling."

NINTH INTERVIEW WITH MRS. B

The major outcome of the interview for Mrs. B was the achievement of some insight into her relationship with Mr. B's family. "I'm not engaged now," she said, and by this she meant that she was no longer obliged to seek constantly to please her in-laws at the cost of stifling her own feelings and impulses, as she had felt she must before marrying and as she has been doing ever since. The interview was essentially an elaboration of this point, and Mrs. B traced the origin of her continued attempts to please her in-laws to her mother's explicit teaching. Mrs. B recalled how good she had felt a short time earlier when she had cleared the air with her sister-in-law by directly expressing her true feelings, without fear.

NINTH INTERVIEW WITH MR. B

Mr. B said at the outset of the interview that he did not know what to talk about, that he felt satisfied in his relationship with Mrs. B and the way their life had been going generally. We explored several aspects of Mr. B's relationship with Mrs. B, and he held steadfastly to his feeling that all was well. With regard to their sexual relationship, Mr. B said he had been so tired recently that he had not been interested in having intercourse, but he reported that Mrs. B had shown an increasing interest in having intercourse. Mr. B commented on the irony of the situation: when Mrs. B had begun to show more interest in sex, he had found that he could not perform with as much sustained zest as he had thought he could. He speculated that perhaps he had experienced a natural decline in sexual prowess.

Mr. B said he truly believed he had become more accepting of Mrs. B: he no longer badgers her to attend to household tasks, nor does he provoke her as he used to do, for example, by silently beginning to wash the dishes when she leaves them in the sink. As a result, he has found that she is not as inadequate as he had thought. Moreover, he and Mrs. B have had a long talk with his sister, and they feel the sister is no longer a destructive force in their lives. Mr. B feels that, all in all, he and Mrs. B love each other more since coming to the agency.

ELEVENTH INTERVIEW WITH MRS. B

Mrs. B manifested positive change in the form of a more balanced attitude toward her relationship with Mr. B: she expressed some negative feelings about him but also freely expressed some of her increasingly positive feelings toward him. She said that it had been too long a time since she had experienced "the good side" of Mr. B, which she feels is now more in evidence. Emphasizing Mrs. B's own increased freedom of expression, I mentioned several occasions on which it had led to more satisfying experiences for her. She told me that after the last joint interview she and Mr. B had talked about the experience amicably, without getting into an argument. Mrs. B said that before coming to the agency she and Mr. B had been incapable of sitting down together and talking something over. Lately, when Mr. B has made barbed jokes about her behavior, she has found herself responding similarly and feeling neither hurt nor resentful afterward, as she did in the past.

THIRTEENTH JOINT INTERVIEW

The B's praised one another for the positive changes that have occurred. Mrs. B spoke of her appreciation of Mr. B's sympathy with her about her impending hospitalization. And he was clearly pleased by her expression of appreciation. Mrs. B spoke of viewing housework not as a chore but as a source of enjoyment because she relates it to her family. Again Mr. B manifested pleasure, saying that he had not previously seen housework in such a light. He added that he no longer felt a desire to do any housework now that he recognized Mrs. B's role; he said that he was finding that Mrs. B could manage the house without his assistance. Mrs. B, in turn, was clearly pleased by her husband's expressions of appreciation. Mr. B said he felt like "a new man."

FOURTEENTH JOINT INTERVIEW

The fact that we were having our final interview was discussed, and both Mr. and Mrs. B expressed satisfaction with our decision.

Several times during the interview Mr. B said he felt he was "in a different world." He feels he has actually matured through examining himself and his marriage in the counseling process. He feels most married couples need some such experience, and he has been encouraging his brother to come to the agency. He feels he has freed himself of his dependency on his mother and her approval and come to realize that his principal concern as an adult should be his own life and his family. He knows he still has some resentment toward his mother, but he pities her more than he resents her. He does not think he needs psychiatric treatment, he said with a smile, because he feels so good about his accomplishment through counseling. Mrs.

B is no longer unduly concerned with winning the approval of Mr. B's mother; she is still interested in her mother-in-law and wants to be on friendly terms, but not at the expense of her own feelings. She no longer holds Mr. B responsible for any friction that arises with her in-laws, but, on the other hand, supports him in relation to his mother and sister.

Mr. B feels different about his work now, as well as about his family relationships. There was a time when he worried excessively about what his customers thought: if a man called and demanded something immediately, Mr. B would work until midnight in order to meet the demand. Now he feels that when a full day's work is done, he wants to go home to his family. Mrs. B was beaming.

The Bolin case was discussed primarily for the purpose of expanding the staff's knowledge of social role theory and its application. The roles of male and female were analyzed. Particular attention was given to the roles of husband and wife and of father and mother and to the effect of role complementarity and role discrepancy on a family's equilibrium. The Bolin case was discussed specifically in terms of the influence on the B's of the role definitions existing in the two families of origin.

The first question raised was whether it was the death of Mr. B's father that precipitated his coming to the agency when he did. It was agreed that his father's death had brought about a shift in Mr. B's role in both his immediate family and his extended family. According to Mr. B's cultural norms, he, as the oldest son, was expected to take responsibility upon his father's death, and Mr. B did take over his father's functions in the business.

There was also a shift in the marital relationship. At the beginning of the marriage Mr. B had worked to build up his wife's ego; she had then begun to develop confidence in herself and in being a woman. Even though the precipitating event that brought Mr. B for help may have been the crisis he experienced at the death of his father, the underlying reason may have been Mrs. B's emotional growth, which threatened him. Although it is more usual for a woman to be the applicant for help, in this case it was the man who experienced greater pain. It was recalled that Mr. B had previously been caught in a situation in which he was fearful of his father and favored by his mother who, together with his sister, dominated him.

What were Mrs. B's expectations from a man and husband? She had idolized her father and considered him to be perfect. He had made the decisions in the family and yet had been tender. Mrs. B had wanted to marry someone like him, and when she had met Mr. B he had reminded her of her father. Without being aware of it, Mrs. B expected her husband to carry the role of father in relation to herself. Since she felt herself to be a daughter to Mr. B, she was unable to help him in building up his self-image as a husband. When she became a mother, much of her tenderness was directed

70

toward her children. Her needs as a woman made her look to men other than her husband for attention.

Mr. B's situation was quite different. He had had a father whom he feared. To him tenderness seemed to be inappropriate to the male role. Yet he had had tenderness from his mother and still needed it. He found a way out of his dilemma by making a joke of the expression of tender feelings. In later years, Mr. B's father disappointed him. Having felt closer to his mother and having been her favorite child, he wanted, first of all, to be a "good son." His mother and sister exploited this impulse of his by trying to control him, and he was pulled between the conflicting roles of son and of husband. His lineal tie, which was strong, stood in the way of the kind of personality development that would have strengthened his marriage. At the same time Mrs. B had developed to the point of becoming ready to fill the role of wife.

Since Mr. B continued to be unsure of his role as a husband and Mrs. B became surer of her role as a wife, their earlier complementarity was disrupted. This upset in the previous marital balance led to dissatisfaction and to Mrs. B's refusal to be active sexually. Another source of trouble was Mr. B's lack of freedom to disagree with his family of orgin, which also shackled Mrs. B. As a daughter-in-law and sister-in-law she felt unable to express herself freely, and her anger over her constraint was displaced onto Mr. B.

When Mr. B became annoyed at Mrs. B's slowness in getting to her housework and her enjoyment of long hours in bed on Sunday mornings, he began to get up early, prepare breakfast, take care of the children, and otherwise assume the role of wife and mother. At the same time he resented the role shift. On her part, Mrs. B was resentful because Mr. B was not firm enough (manly enough?) with the children and left their discipline to her, at times undermining her authority. His behavior was clearly contrary to the behavior Mrs. B viewed as appropriate for the head of the house. At the same time it reflected Mr. B's confusion about what "made a man a man."

When Mr. B's father died, he was somehow shocked into a desire for a better marriage. During the counseling period, Mr. B took definite steps toward asserting his masculinity: he became more outspoken with his mother, affirmed his ability as a good provider, and began to talk over problems with Mrs. B rather than criticize her in a petty way. He no longer took over her housewifely duties when she was "slow." Mrs. B applied herself to her housework with greater zest and got it done without her husband's assistance. She more frequently showed an interest in sexual intercourse and was no longer unduly dependent on her mother-in-law's approval, even though she wanted to be on friendly terms with her. Mr. B came to feel, for the first time, that being a good husband and father was the most important thing in his life; he was able to say so in the last joint interview. Mrs. B was obviously pleased; it was then possible for her to come much closer to her ideal of a wife and mother, since her husband was able to give her both the support she needed and the tenderness she had missed in the past.

3

SYSTEMS THEORY AND THE FUNCTIONS OF MARRIAGE

Otto Pollak

To study the family as a small organization one must first have a solid grounding in the understanding of individual psychodynamics. Once this fundamental knowledge has been acquired, however, the student of the family must make a major shift from dealing with the intrapsychic system to dealing with a system that is created by the interplay of two or more intrapsychic systems. When the caseworker makes this shift, his professional task becomes considerably more complicated. We tend to say that the individual has an environment; under most circumstances the significant parts of an individual's environment are other individuals. The client is viewed as a system, and his environment must be viewed as a number of other systems, with which he, as an intrapsychic system, is interacting. Unless the worker is attuned to these other systems and tries to analyze them, he is likely to center his attention on the individual. When this happens, the more abstractly conceptualized phenomenon—the environment—remains beyond the purview of his diagnostic thinking and therapeutic planning.

THE EXCHANGE PRINCIPLE

A system is operating in every human being, and the essence of its operation is expressed through the alternation of tension and relaxation. Tension can be produced by internal generation without external stimuli; for example, an individual becomes hungry, sleepy, or sexually aroused. These tensions are produced by the system itself. However, tension can also be produced by stimuli from outside the person. In human relationships, a person's tension is usually reduced through exchanges with another human being, so that the tension of one allays the tension of the other through relaxation-producing encounters. This is the ideal form of human interaction, and it is well exemplified by a mother's nursing her child. The mother's tension is created by the purely biological activation of her mammary glands; she feels pressure in her breasts because liquid is accumulating and must be removed. The child comes into the world with a need for the intake of food; his tension is caused by physical hunger. When mother and child come together in the act of nursing, relaxation occurs in the mother's and in the child's biological systems. One can also observe this phenomenon on the emotional level, of course; a mother has the need to nurture her child, the child has the need to be nurtured, and the two produce a gratifying interaction in the encounter. Because of the importance of this phenomenon pediatricians now leave even the defective or brain-damaged child with its mother for about two months of nursing to satisfy the fundamental emotional needs of each.

The exchange principle, of course, may fail to operate because one interactor has nothing to give to the other or because he is unable to give. Ultimately, either circumstance leads to mutual starvation because even the failure of one interactor to give leads eventually to a disappearance of the other's willingness to give. A mother who rejects her child and has a colicky baby is a good example of mutual starvation: the mother does not give the child nourishment in the form in which he can take it, and the child does not keep what she gives him. Both are starved—the mother in her need to have a thriving baby and the baby in his need to have a nurturing mother.

In adulthood, if a person greets another with a smile, convention requires a smile in response. If the smile is not forthcoming, the human interaction loses its exchange character and becomes deprivation. When the exchange principle is violated, starvation or exploitation threatens to destroy the positive quality of any human relationship. For example, many people look forward to a date and then find that they quarrel after five minutes of the actual encounter. They were "stood up," not physically, but emotionally, because they could not give to one another. It is easier to establish contact than to use it constructively. People come to an "emotional dinner," find that they continue to starve, and, after a while, scream at one another. Or one of the two persons in an encounter feels unsatisfied. This one-sided starvation is only an exaggeration of a normal condition, however, because it is almost impossible in human relationships to have exchanges that "come out even."

The concept of relaxation as used here originated in the laboratories of experimental psychologists where, through the observation of external behavior, researchers were able to identify the result of tension reduction in hungry rats. Before finding food, a rat is restless; after finding and eating it, a rat goes to sleep. If one looks for similar behavior sequences in human beings, however, one is likely to be disappointed. In the human being, tension reduction does not result in complete relaxation. Having experienced gratification, he simply gets ready for another tension or begins to perceive another tension. It is apparently inherent in the human condition that very little relaxation is actually experienced. Pervasive relaxation is precluded by the phenomenon of persistent stress, which is generated throughout the entire life of the human being.

In physiology it is assumed that an imperceptible amount of stress always remains. When the human being has had enough stress—after seventy years or so—he is, at least in some measure, ready to die. One can also couch the same idea in psychological terms; every gratification produces the feeling of a permanently lost opportunity for other gratifications. At any point in time, one can have only one gratification, and it forever excludes other gratifications that might have been had at that time.

Human beings go through life permanently tense because relief from one tension sets them free to experience another tension. They also go through life as permanent mourners. We do not dwell on mourning, but we cannot help mourning on an unconscious or a suppressed level. Every day well lived is still a day lost; and it is part of the human adjustment to reduce the extent of the mourning as much as one can and not to become unduly concerned with the unused opportunities of the past. It is a principle of sound mental health that one must strive to accept the loss of one gratification or opportunity as the price to be paid for gaining another.

THE COMPANIONSHIP PRINCIPLE

A second principle to be considered is the companionship principle. This principle is in evidence particularly in a crisis—a condition of change or transition of which we do not know the outcome. What one experiences in a crisis is a longing for companionship, the feeling that one is not alone. Human beings are interdependent, and life can be maintained and improved only through human exchanges. When companionship is absent, a feeling of helplessness overwhelms the person facing a crisis: this becomes particularly clear at certain stages in life, certain periods of transition from one developmental phase to another. Accompanying each such transition—the crisis of adolescence, the crisis of the first pregnancy, the crisis of the menopause, the crisis of retirement, and the crisis of dying—are the feeling that old solutions no longer work and anxiety about finding new solutions.

One of the essential functions of the family is to provide companionship when the human being is going through a crisis. Frequently, however, people feel a need to deny one another companionship in misery; emotionally, they contest the other's mood. The well-known plea, "Don't get angry," addressed to an annoyed person, is unlikely to be helpful. The best thing that one can do is to join the person in his annoyance. The companion, of course, fears that the sufferer's mood will stimulate the same mood in himself. Rather than join the sufferer psychologically, the companion wants to walk away from him, and he expresses this withdrawal in words that signify, "Be another person to me rather than ask me to be like you."

THE ELEMENT OF FATIGUE

Another element of human interaction that deserves mention is the element of fatigue. We have a tendency to assume that things will go on the way they have been going. Two persons who are happily married to each other are supposed to continue to remain happy with one another until death. Actually, even in a good relationship there is an element of unequal stress that can lead to unequal exhaustion, which can lead, in turn, to the severance of the partners' relationship. In such instances there is likely to be social criticism. What others resent is, in part, the arousal of their own anxiety and apprehension lest their own relationships prove not to be as stable and secure as they would like them to be. It is very upsetting to learn that somebody may stop loving and that positive relationships are not secure. What has really happened is that one of the interactors—the one under the greater stress—has reached the point of exhaustion. Inequality of stress should not be viewed as an exceptional circumstance; rather, it can be presumed to be the rule in most human relationships.

THE NEED FOR DESTRUCTION

There is in human interaction not only the need to give and to receive but also the need to destroy and to be destroyed. Mutual gratification of these needs is, of course, much less pleasant to consider than an exchange of support—and the phenomenon has never been genuinely accepted in the United States, with its boundless optimism. When we see somebody being destructive toward another person, we try to find an excuse for the destroyer: he was frustrated, or perhaps his aggression was a reaction to provocation. It is indeed frightening to think that we may want to destroy solely because a human object is available toward whom we can direct our primary aggression. It can be maintained, however, that such primary aggression is at least life-fulfilling because unless we could destroy and ultimately wish to destroy ourselves, we should find it extremely difficult to die. As long as one believes in a life after death, the need to destroy may not be strong. But when one is frightened by the prospect of ultimate extinction, one almost needs as an ally the wish for self-destruction in order to be able to face death.

EXCLUSION AND REJECTION

When more than two persons are involved, a new need is created—the need to make a decision about the person on whom to focus attention. As long as there are only two persons, this need does not arise; one pays attention to the other, and there is no alternative. They may dislike one another, like one another, agree, or disagree; but there is never a problem about whom to accept as interactor. In a triadic or larger group, however, one person becomes the focus of attention: this means that the others are excluded. Such is the problem faced by a married couple when they become parents. Many people believe that the privacy of a dyadic relationship can be ensured by the exclusion of others from attention, and most dyadic relationships operate under this assumption. If the persons interacting belong to any organization, however—be it as small as the family or as large as a university or business corporation—there can be no truly private interaction. In a family, somebody is always watching; and since the watcher is not the focus of attention, he always has to cope with the problem of feeling rejected.

78

One of the great anxieties in family life is the parents' concern about their children's witnessing the primal scene. No matter what the parents do, they are damned. If they go into the privacy of their bedroom and exclude their children, the children react to being excluded. If the children see the act, their feeling of being excluded is even more intense because they are not part of the act and cannot be part of it. When more than two people are involved with one another, privacy does not create immunity against reactions of being excluded. Fantasies of what is happening may replace actual information, but, in such cases, they will determine relevant behavior.

There are, thus, two problems in every group that is composed of more than two members: the problem of deciding on whom to focus attention and, for those who feel themselves not focused on, the problem of coping with the feeling of rejection. It is essential, therefore, for each human being to learn to be rejected without having the feeling of being destroyed. In most instances the association of rejection with destruction is based on the transference of infantile anxieties to adult situations. Learning to discriminate between childhood associations and adult experience is essential. "Working through the transference" is not confined to psychoanalysis; it is the ever-renewed task of learning to cope with life.

The individual is helped to accomplish this task if he can gain a sense of structure within the complexity of group life. It becomes bearable to a person not to be the focus of attention in a large group if he has had adequate support in similar experiences in small, more intimate groups. A relatively stable distribution of power is of help. Lacking it, each person has to restructure each new situation, and such restructuring is very stressful. There is a kind of unconscious wisdom in the fact that the father is the most important person in some families, and the mother, in others. Democratic principles, however, frequently spill over into family life when it is felt that the family should reflect political ideals of equality. This circumstance denies the legitimacy of arrangements of superordination and subordination. In reality, the family is an organization of unequals, for family members are different from one another in terms of age, sex, and degree of development. There is, therefore, a power structure. In older family models the power structure was felt to be legitimate; now it is being questioned. Such questioning of the family power structure is conducive to rebellion, as can be seen in the behavior of today's adolescents.

A schema of marital interaction can be developed without difficulty because the operation of the exchange principle in marriage is generally accepted. But if one wants to develop a similar schema for what parents and children do for one another, or should do for one another, one encounters a strange difficulty. My study of the literature suggests that the relationships between parents and children are largely described and analyzed by lovers of children, who emphasize only what the parents should do or do not do for the children; they pay little attention to what the children should do for the parents. If one identifies with children, one may become a child psychiatrist, a child welfare worker, or a child psychologist. It is interesting to note that no specialization has ever been created for service to parents; there are no parent psychiatrists, only child psychiatrists. The terminology betrays the identification—and the implication is that parents are important factors in the rearing of children but not of sufficient importance in themselves to warrant a professional specialization. It is, therefore, easier to discuss in detail the marital relationship, because more information about this kind of interaction is available.

THE MARITAL SYSTEM

In essence, there are four phases in marriage, separated from each other by crises of transition—and for every crisis situation one can invariably identify the function of the spouse as that of a companion in, rather than a contestant of, moods. Each of the four phases is characterized by a change in family structure.

The first phase is lived out before the birth of children.

The second is the period during which the children are at home.

The third is the period of the children's adolescence, while they are leaving the home. Nor is the period of the children's departure a short one. Middle-class families in the United States, for example, accept college education as a necessity for their children, and the children frequently live away from home while attending college. The separation of children from their parents starts with the freshman year of the first child and ends with the senior year of the last one. In between, of course, the children come home for vacations only so that they can go away again, to camp or to Europe! Thus, the period of marital life during which the children are leaving the home constitutes for the parents a long period of installment mourning over separations. And although the picture presented is that of middle-class life, it is essentially the model desired by people of lower-class status, too. One of the most outstanding phenomena supporting the theory of the mass distribution of our model arrangements is the fact that Americans are not visibly distinguished from one another by the quality of their clothes. (In Europe people reveal their class by the clothes they wear.) Some women pay $500 for essentially the same dress for which other women pay $39.95. But the dresses do not look so different; the woman who pays more merely has a greater feeling of satisfaction from knowing that she has paid a high price. The middle-class model is presented on the assumption that other classes want it, too. Actually, only the middle-class person questions the middle-class model. Lower-class persons also want to have their children go to college, to camp, and to Europe.

Finally, the fourth phase in marriage is the one that follows the departure of all the children; a private interactional relationship between the marital partners is re-established, without the bloom that accrued from early fantasies. In many ways the aging period is the ultimate testing ground of the partners' coping capacities, because this is frequently a period of declining health.

INTERPERSONAL REORIENTATION

Interpersonal reorientation is an important thread that can be followed through each of the four phases of marriage. It can be seen clearly in the first phase, when each partner has to shift from seeing a parent as the person most important to him to seeing the spouse as most important. Some persons never make the shift. In a healthy relationship, however, spouses think of one another first in moments of crisis and do not wish to go back to mother or father, even in fantasy. Nevertheless, one must not demand too high a level of maturity from one's partner and must permit him an occasional nonpathological regression, for one of the essential elements of a good marital relationship is the provision of an opportunity for satisfaction of the need to revisit one's childhood. To permit such an occasional regression, the marriage partners must be tolerant of one another. If they are lucky, they will have similar wishes in this respect, and then they can go visiting their childhood together. But not all partners can be so well matched, and each must still be able to accept his partner's regression and possibly give him reassurance if he feels guilty about giving expression to it.

There is great security in having one's marital partner as a primary resource, particularly in an emergency. This is best illustrated, perhaps, by the statement of one client to the effect that she could not stand living with her husband but that she experienced a feeling of security when she woke up at night and heard him breathing in the next bed. Furthermore, during the first phase of marriage the development of a spectrum of shared interests is inevitable. This, in itself, can frequently lead to a feeling of love where none existed. Most people complain that they cannot love somebody whom they feel obliged to love; but if marital partners can become more like one another, their need to love will find fulfillment. Ultimately, most persons love those who are similar to themselves, and one of the ways of making oneself loved and loving is to increase the similarities between oneself and the other. If there are sufficient areas in which similarities can develop, a certain liking for one another must result. And marriage is an excellent setting for the development of similarities. It was the wisdom of the Jewish marriage that it was arranged, for it was arranged on the basis of similarities between the two people. The marriage broker knew that when people similar to one another are brought together, affection is likely to grow. And he was adept at identifying similarities; otherwise he could not have stayed in business. Computer-arranged dates are based on the same idea.

When the first child is born, the spouses must go through a second interpersonal reorientation. Each partner must permit the other to have an additional love object. Hardly have the spouses managed to reorient themselves from parent to spouse when they have to permit the spouse to relate himself to another person. This is the point at which consideration must be given to what children do for parents. The baby not only releases the tension in the mother's breast; he also represents the father's first step toward immortality. To the father he is verification of his virility, possibly a shield against whatever anxiety he may have about aging, and a proof that he has fulfilled social expectations. For all these reasons there is an immediate bond between father and child, which lessens the mother's monopolistic hold on her husband; but, at the moment, she is so much the center of attention that she may not think about it.

Filling the parental role imposes a restriction on the parents' regressive satisfactions. One can be much more childlike with one's spouse before the arrival of children. This is one of the unacknowledged reasons for a couple's postponing the first attempts at procreation. Parenthood demands increasingly adult behavior because it carries with it a protective, rearing function. At the same time, the child's impulse freedom stimulates the parents' regressive urges. In this respect each spouse must support the other as he deals with the tension created by simultaneously being forced to be more adult and stimulated to be more childlike. One of the risks of single parenthood is the absence of another adult to give support in this struggle.

In the third phase interpersonal reorientation of the marriage partners involves the experience of mourning. There is, of course, mourning over the children's leaving. But there are other mournings that are frequently not considered. During the man's career, there almost invariably comes a time when he has to recognize that he is not going to fulfill his fantasies about advancement. Recruiters for large corporations frequently give college graduates the promise of advancement to top positions. At twenty-two years of age, a young man is treated as if he is a future president of the corporation; when he is thirty-five he begins to realize that he will never be even a vice-president, but he has to continue living. Mourning over having to give up one's fantasies of achievement is part and parcel of almost everyone's life and requires marital support and empathy.

Another cause for mourning in the third phase of marriage is the climacteric. This is usually a more pronounced cause for mourning in women than in men, since the climacteric in men is more blurred. Husbands must function as companions to their wives in relation to menopausal experiences.

In this phase of a marriage, moreover, the couple's spectrum of interests becomes smaller. People who cannot accept the narrowing of the spectrum sometimes produce a second crop of children, if this is physiologically possible; doing so may represent an unconscious refusal to enter the declining phase of life.

In the last phase of marriage each spouse must help the other prepare for being the survivor. Since men, on the average, die sooner than women, it is more the husband's obligation to prepare his wife to be the survivor. This is, of course, very difficult because it is anxiety-creating to think of one's own death. It also requires a certain giving up of one's own wish to be desirable. But one must permit the other partner to develop other interests, which will last when one is gone. Everything that is vital in oneself works against doing this. One wants to be the most important person and resents competing with a variety of other interests; one does not want to deteriorate or give up one's own lovability. But the most egotistical thing one can do in a marriage is to make oneself intensely desirable at a time when there is a reasonable chance that one will not survive the partner. Most men succeed in spite of themselves—they become disagreeable even though they do not want to be disagreeable. And the wives develop other interests even when the husbands want to be their only interest.

SOME CONCLUDING OBSERVATIONS

In the sexual sphere, marital partners encounter the very difficult task of helping one another in ethical reorientation. Since sexual experience begins

82

very early in life, long before marriage can even be conceived of, sex, for many people, remains associated with the forbidden. Consequently, one of the tasks of the partners is to prepare each other for the legitimacy of an experience that at an earlier stage was associated with prohibition. This frequently can be done only at the price of some feeling of disenchantment, because the fun of the forbidden is a powerful force. The monopolistic power, or monopolistic claim, of the American marriage is dynamically dangerous because it carries with it an experience of disappointment. At the same time this claim makes adultery both doubly forbidden and doubly attractive. Other societies provide some outlet—concubinage or a double standard—but one of the prices of equality between the sexes is the conviction that marriage is the only relationship within which sex should be expressed. Thus Americans frequently suffer more from the morality of the marriage system than do people in other cultures that have different systems. And thus, in the United States, a variety of family services had to come into existence because of the demands made on the institution of marriage. The greater the demands, the fewer the people who will be able to meet them.

An even more subtle interplay in marriage is the interaction between the partners' two sets of defenses. Frequently one person's defenses pierce the defenses of the other, so that a tremendous amount of vulnerability to the return of the repressed is created through the intimacy of the relationship. A good human relationship between two people should be strengthening for both, and their interaction should make them feel that they are becoming more adequate in coping and are dependable resources for one another.

Finally, damage can be done to a marriage relationship by a difference in the level of psychosexual development of the partners and by inability to assist one another in learning the social roles required by the aging process. The essence of a good human relationship is violated when the persons involved are weakened by it rather than strengthened. If a healthy relationship is to endure, the executive as well as the defensive functions of the ego of each marriage partner must be strengthened through the marital interaction.

In the discussion that followed Dr. Pollak's presentation, the chief concern was the human problems created by society's changing expectations of the individual. In theory, our society expects the man to be strong, aggressive, and dominant and the woman to be soft, gentle, and passive. In reality, however, the clear-cut complementarity suggested by these contrasting qualities rarely exists. One of the main reasons seems to be that our educational system serves to blur sexual differences. From the beginning of life and throughout the early years of formal schooling, boys are nurtured almost exclusively by women and have little opportunity to identify with strong masculine figures who can be observed doing clearly masculine work.

On the other hand, our educational practices deny girls the opportunity and the right to be soft and gentle; they are trained implicitly, and sometimes explicitly, to be strong and aggressive. Thus both sexes are taught to respond to ambivalent signals, and a true sexual complementarity based on clear-cut differences becomes increasingly difficult to achieve.

Mention was made of the potentialities for stress caused by the incompatibility between the traditional model of the family as a refuge for its members—a place where regression in defense of the ego is not only possible but also appropriate—and society's implied demand that adult family members always act in a mature fashion.

Out of these considerations came the suggestion that caseworkers should redefine their model of the family. As a result of such a redefinition, treatment goals should become more realistic. The caseworker should not impose his own goals on clients. He should help marital partners and family members achieve a complementarity that is wholesome for them and attainable by them; doing so involves recognition that the family can sometimes serve as an appropriate setting for regression.

Some members of the discussion group disagreed with Dr. Pollak's view that in old age it is easier for the surviving spouse to give up the other spouse to death if the negative aspects of the marital relationship have become dominant. Is it true that it is easier for the surviving spouse to involve himself in new relationships and activities if he is able to view his former partner as having become less satisfactory? Some members expressed the belief that the opposite may be true: if the needs of the marriage partners have been adequately met and the relationship has remained positive, there is greater ease in moving into new relationships. Would a person's general outlook on life also affect his attitude toward the loss of the partner in old age?

During one of the two study sessions based on Dr. Pollak's presentation, the observation was made that he had brought together many of the ideas that had been considered earlier in the seminar, specifically, facets of crisis and role theory. As reference was made to his emphasis on the large amount of stress to which human life is subjected, the meaning and effect of cultural factors were mentioned. Part of our tension seems to arise from the need of the individual continually to make decisions and choices because there is no firmly established social pattern. Also, our society stresses "producing," and tension is created when one feels that he is not sufficiently productive.

Another source of stress mentioned by Dr. Pollak seemed to the discussants to be particularly important, the mourning of lost opportunities. This seems almost inevitable as one increasingly recognizes that he will never be able to achieve everything he wants, that he will never realize all his dreams, and that he will never function in all the areas in which he might possibly have been active. Settling for what is—striking the balance we must strike with increasing urgency as we get older—cannot be done without paying a price in sadness and regret for what will never be. How many clients come to our agency primarily because of the nagging pain caused by a failure to achieve what they wanted to achieve!

Mention was made of failures in human exchange that frequently come

84

to light in casework practice: mutual starvation and one-sided giving, which lead to emotional fatigue; and a more restricted play of fantasy as the necessity for settling down to face reality becomes more compelling with age. There was some disagreement with Dr. Pollak's emphasis on the importance of seeing one's existence as becoming less and less attractive toward the end, and it was suggested that "belief and faith" might act as support to the person facing the approach of death.

Another point that caused considerable discussion was Dr. Pollak's view that people who are similar to each other have a better chance of making a successful marriage. It was thought that his position might be valid in regard to values and general life goals, but doubt was expressed about its validity in regard to temperament, intelligence, and personality structure.

The casework experience of the staff was tapped in relation to the marital role-carrying in the modern family, and a number of conclusions were reached. It is the exceptional family in which the husband-father is the undisputed head of the household. In most families decision-making and leadership are shared by husband and wife in accordance with the kind of complementarity they have developed. Not infrequently, in families coming for counseling help, marital roles have been reversed. In our casework practice, our main question has been: "Does the particular role behavior of the partners work for *this* family?" When the answer to this question is in the affirmative, we are most likely to accept the family's pattern and not to be concerned about some ideal model of "what should be." Usually our major concern in such instances is the effect on the child. How does his parents' lack of clarity in role, or role reversal, affect his understanding of *his* role? There is no doubt that he can benefit from a successfully balanced, though deviating, parental relationship, but only insofar as it does not confuse him to the extent that he cannot define his own sexual identity, particularly in adolescence.

Role definitions are not static; they change as society changes. Sometimes societal demands are contradictory and decisions about appropriate role behavior have to be made, both individually and collectively. Undoubtedly, the caseworker's own values are constantly operating in his counseling, and one of his most pressing obligations is to be aware of his own values and his own beliefs about desirable family models.

Biologically, the roles of the two sexes are quite distinct. But our sedentary way of life and our use of the machine have altered our concept of masculinity, and economic and educational developments have altered our concept of femininity. Our definitions have become subtler, and they differ in different social classes and subcultures. The Jewish middle class emphasizes the fulfillment of individual potential, for both man and woman, and the same emphasis appears to be characteristic of the American middle class in general. Perhaps in the future there will be less social criticism of the "softer" male and of the stronger, less pliable female. There being no firm general definitions of male and female roles in today's American society, the caseworker must raise various questions about each family that comes for help: (1) How much satisfaction do the husband and the wife derive from the way they define and carry their roles? (2) In what specific ways is the children's growth furthered or impeded by the manner in which the parents carry their roles? (3) Does the model adopted by the family strengthen or weaken its coping capacity? Casework help in effecting changes and establishing a different balance should be offered principally when roles are carried in a way that does not work satisfactorily for the couple or in a way that constitutes a danger for the children.

There was considerable discussion about whether or not caseworkers have an obligation to represent society and, therefore, to attempt to help families adapt to a model that society seems to favor. Since the assumption that each family must adapt to a predetermined social model is in conflict with the acceptance of individual choice as a social value, the social work profession must take initiative in deciding which social values (within a wide range of values) will be given precedence. This is a difficult, though important, task, since society's mandates and models are ambiguous and are constantly changing.

THE BRENNER CASE*

Mr. B, aged 21 years, chemist
Mrs. B, aged 20 years, college junior
Son, aged 2 months

On October 23, Mrs. B telephoned the agency and spoke to the receptionist. She referred to a former contact (in a family life education session) with one of the agency's counselors. Since then she had been married; she had a two-month-old baby; and she was in the process of getting a divorce. She was attending night school one evening a week and hoped to get her bachelor's degree eventually. She asked for help in finding evening and Saturday work.

The case was assigned to me, the former contact to whom Mrs. B had referred.

OCTOBER 28

I telephoned Mrs. B, and she was obviously relieved that I was the person to call her. I told her I realized that, under the circumstances, it took a lot of courage for her to call; she was most appreciative and said that my awareness of her distress made it much easier for her to talk to me. She had come to realize that her marriage had been impulsive, and, in effect, defiance. She said she did not want an appointment, having called to ask for help in finding a job, but I felt quite certain that she had wanted to find out indirectly whether or not I would be ready to see her again. She said that since she had phoned she had made arrangements to work at night and on Saturdays doing office work and that her situation had thus become much more manageable. I said I was glad for her.

NOVEMBER 14

Numerous telephone calls and messages were received from Mrs. B. She called first to request an appointment, then to cancel it, then to request that the appointment be rescheduled, then to say that she was definitely through with the marriage, and finally to say that she wanted an appointment because if there was one chance in a million of salvaging the marriage, she wanted to find out. Mr. B also called and conveyed his ambivalence and uncertainty about what to do. We arranged an appointment. In the telephone contact he indicated to me that his lawyer had suggested that he and Mrs. B both come to the agency and that they be seen separately; he was following his lawyer's suggestion. After Mrs. B had cancelled her original appointment, Mr. B telephoned to say that he knew of her decision and wondered whether his appointment still stood. On learning that he

* Submitted by Mrs. Mollie Spector.

wanted to keep it, I assured Mr. B of my readiness to see him as planned. He seemed greatly relieved.

NOVEMBER 18

Since Mrs. B had insisted she wanted to see me by herself, I was greatly surprised to see Mr. B appear with his wife at her appointment time. Since they both requested to be seen together and since I felt it might be the more productive approach to their problem, I agreed.

Mrs. B, who is still an attractive girl, appeared to have gained weight since I had last seen her. She wore dark glasses during most of the interview. Mr. B is a very boyish, rather intelligent young man, somewhat passive and dependent. It was quickly clear to me that his stake in the marriage was considerably more than Mrs. B's; her behavior was manipulative and impulsive, and she clearly conveyed her need to be right and more knowledgeable than her husband.

I mentioned my surprise at their coming together. I said I was aware of their marked ambivalence about their marriage. Like two children they acknowledged I was right in judging them to be ambivalent; yet both of them said their prime purpose in coming was to try to salvage the marriage. I made it clear I could not tell them then whether or not the marriage could be salvaged. Certainly their previous behavior, which had been triggered by Mrs. B's impulsiveness, would have to be examined in terms of what the marriage really meant to each of them. Mrs. B was struck by my statement —almost as if she had thought that, merely by coming and making the request, she had guaranteed that the marriage would be saved. Mr. B's reaction was not as evident.

Though Mrs. B briefly tried to hide the fact—when I told her I was aware of her pattern of impulsiveness—discussion revealed that she had been two months' pregnant when she and Mr. B had married. It helped them both to know that I had known Mrs. B prior to their marriage and had some knowledge of her way of handling situations. Mrs. B spoke about the beginning of the marriage, including her pregnancy; she spoke of the insecurity of her husband's employment and of the need for her to work part time to augment his income. With much implicit criticism, she said she had been able to work only part time because of her nausea. Mr. B reacted defensively; Mrs. B persisted in making her point; and Mr. B retreated. The relationship had been much less idyllic than either of them had expected. On the basis of both their accounts, and particularly Mr. B's, I began to question whether their feelings for each other were as positive as they claimed, and I suggested that perhaps they were both reaching out for their families as the important persons in their lives. I recalled Mrs. B's telling me that her family had fully accepted Mr. B into their household and had indeed fostered and encouraged an early marriage. Mr. B said he had been aware that his closeness to Mrs. B's family had constituted a kind of rebellion against his own family, but he also said he had felt threatened by being swallowed up by them and had then retreated somewhat and moved back into a more positive relationship with his parents. At that time he had discussed his whole career and his marriage with them, and he felt he had achieved a much firmer connection with his father particularly. Together, we pondered the question whether the marriage relationship had ever really had a chance of success, particularly because of the possessive way in which Mrs. B's parents had accepted Mr. B.

Mr. B indicated that his parents fought a great deal, but said that they did so openly. Mrs. B said she feared that her husband was attempting to pattern their marriage after that of his parents, and we then talked about the naturalness of such an approach. Mrs. B maintained that her parents' marriage was so perfect that she wanted to emulate it—and I made some comments about conflicts' sometimes being kept under cover. The point I stressed was that Mr. and Mrs. B's marriage would be what they made it, and I suggested that they cease fighting for control and domination.

It was plain that the couple had reconciled, but I was strongly aware that Mrs. B was going through motions of reconciliation rather than make an emotional investment in it. Mr. B was more committed to the marriage. I offered the possibility of seeing them a few times for the purpose of trying to determine together whether or not the marriage was salvageable; I said I could offer no guarantees. I felt Mrs. B's withdrawal as I said this. Then, with marked hesitation, she said she wanted to know whether I would tell her and Mr. B, after a few appointments, if I felt the marriage could not work. I told them I felt they would know for themselves. I spoke directly to Mrs. B about her lack of commitment really to work on the marriage; Mr. B brought out the fact that her divorce action was still pending. Mrs. B shot him a furious look, and I again pointed out that she did not seem ready to make a real investment in trying to salvage the marriage. A very full discussion of the issue followed—and I felt Mr. B was much more realistic about investing work in the marriage than was Mrs. B. In the face of his position, she could not hold her own. She offered assurances that she would drop the divorce action and try to work on the marriage. Though doubtful of her commitment, I felt I must accept it. I scheduled two separate interviews with each of them and then three joint appointments. There was a clear understanding among us that by the end of the interview program we had planned, they would know just what the chances were of working out their marriage successfully. There was agreement that we would examine particularly the basis of the marriage and the nature of the positive elements in the relationship. There is a child.

NOVEMBER 26 THROUGH MAY 22, SIX-MONTH SUMMARY

Six joint interviews were held with Mr. and Mrs. B; five individual interviews with Mr. B; sixteen with Mrs. B; and one with Mrs. B's mother, Mrs. C. There were also various telephone calls, several from Mrs. C. The first phase of the contact can be construed as ending on January 31, the date on which Mr. and Mrs. B separated.

In my interviews with Mrs. B she was guarded, fearful of facing her feelings about her husband. Gradually, however, she began to examine the significance of the fact that there was little she could say she liked about her husband. It appeared that Mr. and Mrs. B competed with each other in terms of competence and domination of the relationship. Mrs. B fought

Mr. B in many ways, primarily through withdrawal and passive resistance. There was no area in their relationship that seemed to offer either of them any real satisfaction. Mrs. B realized that she had perhaps become pregnant in order to embarrass her parents, though she continued to maintain that she "adored" them. Examining her relationship with her parents in a very superficial way, she began to see her father as having been a weak person and her mother as the one who had cracked the whip and made all the decisions. She found herself to be behaving in very much the same fashion, even though she pretended she did not like the results of her behavior. Ultimately Mrs. B acknowledged the fact that she really did not want the marriage. But she did not want to take responsibility for making the decision that it should be terminated; she wanted me to do so for her. She was afraid to decide against the marriage for fear she might be wrong; at the same time she was afraid to choose the marriage, for fear she would lose her identity as an individual and be dominated by her husband.

Concurrently Mr. B was trying to deny the pain for him in the relationship, even while it was being evidenced by the flare-up of a dermatological disorder of the hands. Though Mr. B had previously evaded a dermatologist's suggestion that the condition might have its root in emotional problems, he acknowledged to me that he was risking more expression of his feelings with his wife—particularly the tender ones—because he wanted the marriage very much. He saw, however, that he harped on certain topics and bore down very heavily on his wife; his hostility was reinforced by the fact that Mrs. B had not severed her connection with the lawyer she had contacted about a divorce, even though she spoke about reconciliation. Mr. B could not see her position as evidence of lack of commitment, but chose to see it as obstinacy, saying she persistently opposed him in everything. He was miserable because his wife was becoming careless about her physical appearance—gaining a lot of weight—and was slovenly about the house. Mr. B, however, had also not ended his contact with his lawyer in the divorce action. Gradually Mr. B acknowledged there was really no hope of salvaging the marriage because whatever efforts they were making to do so were merely superficial. He felt, but could not admit, that his wife was growing more distant from him. His own fear of failure and his fear of repeating the pattern of unhappy marriage he saw in his parents' home shook him deeply.

Mr. B used me extensively in his desperate effort to save the marriage—while it was clear that he and Mrs. B were incompatible and the relationship so negative that there was little chance that it could be saved. He telephoned me frequently and had two emergency appointments. When he phoned on January 29, asking to be seen immediately, he was in tears because he and Mrs. B had reached the decision that they had to separate. He protested that he still loved his wife and would make every effort to try to win her back. I tried to help Mr. B see some of the positive elements in the dissolution of the relationship, which offered neither partner any satisfaction. He resisted all my positive suggestions, and later he became quite bitter.

Mr. B revealed a considerable amount of background that bore on his current situation. His family was, and had always been, poor. At one time he had been in business for himself but had had to give up the business and now had a job in which he was unhappy. His life had been miserable. Mr. B said that his father, though only forty-four years of age, looked and acted like a man of sixty-four; his mother was a fanatic about cleanliness. He seemed to place women in a position of inferiority in relation to men. He spoke of a number of occasions on which his mother and father were nearly divorced. He has one brother who was graduated from high school but is still not vocationally established. Claiming that he himself had been graduated from high school at seventeen years of age, Mr. B said he had gone to college but quit because he had been "over his head" academically. He had left home after he left college and lived alone: his father was too domineering; it was impossible to talk with him in a reasonable way. Mr. B acknowledged that he had no real image of a husband—and he saw that he was afraid to give to his wife because of his need to dominate her; he mentioned that his father had often told him that his guard was always up.

Mr. B's conflicted feelings about his wife were manifest. He alternated between saying that he had married her because he thought that she would make a good mother and a good housekeeper and saying that she was a failure in both respects. He expressed great resentment against her parents for their willingness to take her back whenever she felt inclined to leave him. He resented, too, their greater financial means, with which he felt they could entice his wife away from him; at the same time he seemed to feel guilty about having benefited himself, in a calculated way, by their financial resources. It was obvious that Mrs. B's mother had had a hand in disrupting the marriage. Mr. B manifested some feeling of guilt about his premarital sexual relations with his wife but also argued in some detail that it was her planning that had resulted in her pregnancy; he acknowledged that he had some responsibility but continued to stress the fact that she had maneuvered him into spending a long week end with her in a hotel. In many ways Mr. B felt that he was the rescuer, that he was liberating Mrs. B from a home situation in which she had no opportunity to express herself.

Mrs. B could accept some responsibility for having become pregnant before the marriage and said she felt that in doing so she had been in some measure retaliating against her parents. She had, actually, little experience in dating, whereas her husband had considerable capacity socially; she concurred with his description of her as a girl who did not make friends easily and was inordinately shy, in spite of excellent academic achievement. Mr. B enjoyed Mrs. B's family but at the same time disliked being dependent on them; he was well aware, as was Mrs. B, that her parents used the young couple's financial dependence to keep them tied close, particularly at the beginning of the marriage when the B's lived with them. Both Mr. and Mrs. B spoke of arguing about picayune things, in a way that seemed to reflect Mrs. B's impulsiveness and Mr. B's increasing bitterness and hostility. Dependence on Mrs. B's family obviously distressed Mr. B; it seemed to me that Mrs. B had been fully aware of his distress but done nothing to alter the situation. The birth of the baby had triggered more conflict, and Mr.

and Mrs. B felt that they must move away from the C's home to try to straighten out their relationship. They had no funds; Mr. B's family could give very little; Mrs. B's family gave more, but they also held on tightly to the couple.

According to Mrs. B, in their interaction, Mr. B devalued her and gave her no credit for her accomplishments. Her own immaturity was quite obvious. The relationship deteriorated steadily, and though I tried to hold the couple to a plan to come to a decision about their marriage as objectively as possible during a series of four appointments, they decided to separate just before the end of the period. The move gave some relief to Mrs. B, who had recognized in some measure in the course of the interviews that if she had waited, she would not have married her husband; she acknowledged her disappointment in herself and her anger with herself because of her impulsiveness.

During the upheaval of the separation, which lasted with some violence for several weeks, Mrs. C telephoned me twice, wanting directions from me about how to deport herself. I asked if she wanted to come to the agency to discuss the matter with me, but she demurred. Over the telephone I could do no more than advise her not to interfere because the couple had to make the decision whether to try to salvage the marriage or to terminate it. I did not express my own estimate of the situation to Mrs. C—that her daughter did not want the marriage, though she did not want to take the responsibility for ending it, and that Mr. B's motives for wanting to maintain it were unsound.

After the separation I saw Mr. B and offered to see him further over a period of time to try to help him make the adjustment to the separation and to build a life for himself again. But he did not continue for the proposed period of time although he ended in a responsible way. His hurt was real and his confusion touching. He was also bitter and spoke much of retaliating in the future. I was able to help him resolve some of his distress, and although he was still unhappy at the time of our last appointment, he had begun to reconcile himself to the idea of divorce.

My work with Mrs. B after the separation was much more extensive. She had returned to her parents' home, which was not easy for her because she had begun to glimpse some of her mother's controlling pattern and was afraid of slipping back into her former compliant relationship with her. We discussed the possibility of her living elsewhere by herself, but it was not practical for her to do so, at least at that time. Mrs. B asked for continuing appointments, saying she wanted to sort out some of her feelings and plan a future for herself. She made excellent use of our relationship. She came to see much more clearly how she had lent herself to her mother's manipulation, out of her need to be liked by her. She saw that her father was indeed a weak person; she saw, moreover, that the small amount of strength he had, had been nullified by Mrs. C's overbearing control. The fact that Mrs. B's sister had, even while living at home, liberated herself in some measure from her mother's control, gave Mrs. B the courage to decide to do likewise. In the course of trying to free herself from her mother's domination, Mrs. B developed a much closer and more wholesome and satisfying relationship with her sister. Feeling threatened by the danger that her daughters would form an alliance against her, Mrs. C asked for an appointment with me, ostensibly to discuss ways of helping Mrs. B to become more independent while she was living at home. I confronted Mrs. C mildly with her manipulation of the relationships in the family and then offered her further help in determining how much responsibility she should take for Mrs. B, but she declined a future appointment.

Mrs. C's refusal to become genuinely involved had the effect of supporting Mrs. B in her efforts to grow up. She evidenced in many small but meaningful ways an increasing ability to make decisions about the child, about her use of her very small income, and about the divorce. She carried through the divorce action, selling her engagement ring to finance it rather than become indebted to her mother. Beyond that, Mrs. B used the support money her husband paid for the child to meet the child's needs and worked out an arrangement with her parents whereby they gave her a small amount of money in return for her assumption of various housekeeping responsibilities.

As Mrs. B's insight increased, she was able to take steps slowly but surely toward building her future life. She went back to school, and she also went out on a date. At the same time, however, she was unable to lose the weight she had gained after her marriage; she ultimately sought the help of a physician, but it was not effective.

Mrs. B's self-respect increased as she became aware of her growing ability to think and act without being dependent on her mother's approval and permission, as she had been formerly. She also began to develop a relationship with her father. When I last saw her, she had taken a part-time job working for him temporarily and was keeping her earnings for herself, much to Mrs. C's consternation. Mrs. B was somewhat gleeful as she recognized more and more her mother's attempts to manipulate and control and her own ability to assert herself without becoming upset. She began to feel capable of carrying on without the support of the somewhat dependent relationship she had developed with me. As we discussed the matter thoroughly, Mrs. B achieved the meaningful realization that she had grown in the course of our relationship and that she was free to end it.

At the beginning of the discussion of the Brenner case, one staff member suggested that the recorded statement of the worker, "There is a child," implied a predisposition on her part to try to keep the couple from terminating their marriage. The opinion was expressed by another participant that counseling should afford marital partners an opportunity to discover for themselves whether they want to remain together or separate, that the presence of children should not preclude an honest evaluation of pros and cons in the marriage.

An examination of the forces operating to bring Mr. and Mrs. B together before marriage led to the conclusion that, by and large, those forces were negative. Although Mrs. B was physically attracted to Mr. B, the choice of Mr. B as her mate was really made by her parents, whose acceptance and approval were essential to her. At the same time, Mrs. B unconsciously wanted to separate from her parents and established her relationship with Mr. B as a means of effecting a separation from them. Mr. B, by his own admission, had been exposed to a poor example of marriage inasmuch as his parents had been near divorce.

Conflicting social attitudes toward premarital pregnancy were discussed: On the one hand, society holds an individual responsible for his behavior; on the other hand, prevailing attitudes imply that a male is not a "real man" if he is not sexually aggressive when he has the opportunity to be so. One participant suggested that social attitudes are based on a recognition of the differences between male and female sexual responses and that society therefore views the woman as the responsible party in at least some instances of presumed seduction. Another participant expressed the view that when a couple is engaged to be married, as were the B's when Mrs. B became pregnant, society expects the man to take responsibility for avoiding a pregnancy. Although there was some disagreement regarding the kind of behavior society does expect in such a situation, there was consensus that the complexity of social norms, and the fact that they are frequently incompatible, can lead the individual to behave in a manner that is frustrating to him as he experiences the censure of society.

As the B case was analyzed, these marital partners were described as two adolescents who had gone from adolescence to parenthood without ever having become adults in the true sense. They had not had the opportunity either to grow to adulthood or to grow into the roles of husband and wife; they were completely unprepared to assume the roles of father and mother— to give up any of their own satisfactions in order to nurture a child. Mrs. B's pregnancy had not resulted from a wish for a child, but from impulsive rebellion against a stifling tie to her mother. The mother, in turn, had used the pregnancy as a means of binding Mrs. B more closely to her and preventing the normal process of separation.

Various psychological concepts were discussed, including failure to differentiate between reality and fantasy: people frequently enter upon important life experiences—marriage, for example—with certain fixed fantasies about what the experience will be like and then find it ncessary in the course of the actual experience to differentiate the reality from the fantasy. It appeared that the B's had been unable to do so. Another concept discussed was the necessity for a person to have accepted his own individuality and growth process in order to be able to accept the growth of another person.

Five types of neurotic marital interaction were reviewed as a backdrop for an examination of the interaction between Mr. and Mrs. B: (1) sadism-masochism; (2) a demand for love by one partner met by emotional detachment of the other; (3) a mutual struggle for dominance; (4) one partner's plea of helplessness, as he looks upon the other as the rescuer who can provide magical protection; and (5) alternation between dependency and self-assertion in each.[1]

The B's interaction was viewed as an example of the mutual struggle for dominance. Both appeared to be more preoccupied with saving their fantasies than with saving their marriage. Reference was made to a cultural bias according to which the woman is favored and viewed as "the victim" in such a situation. Staff discussion tended to focus on Mrs. B, whose illegitimate pregnancy and pronounced dependency seemed to overshadow Mr. B's needs and suffering. The counselor who had carried the case reminded the participants of Mr. B's dependency, which had obstructed his growth, and of his deep suffering during the process of separation. The view was expressed that Mr. and Mrs. B, both engaged in a struggle to separate from their own parents, were seeking substitute parents in their marriage and were disappointed because neither was ready to assume a parental role for the other. The suggestion was also made that Mr. B may have been unconsciously "marrying" his own mother in the form of his mother-in-law, who had taken such an active role in courting him for her daughter.

Mrs. B's selling her ring to pay for the divorce action, rather than taking money from her mother for this purpose, was thought to be evidence that she had indeed grown through the use of counseling help. Whereas Mrs. B's separation from her mother had been initially established as a goal by the counselor, Mrs. B was so gratified by the result of counseling that she made the goal her own. The point was made that implicit in such counseling is the need for the worker to be constantly aware of his own feelings and values; since it is impossible to be neutral in the realm of values, the real challenge to the counselor is to prevent his own values from interfering with the helping relationship and to use them in the way that will be of most benefit to the client.

[1] Bela Mittelmann, "Analysis of Reciprocal Neurotic Patterns in Family Relationships," *Neurotic Interaction in Marriage*, Victor W. Eisenstein (ed.), Basic Books, New York, 1956, pp. 81–100.

4

IRISH AND JEWISH FAMILY VALUES AND TODAY'S REALITY

Otto Pollak

Any analysis of family life in the United States must take note of cultural and subcultural variations. And every client of a family service agency brings with him into the office of the caseworker the history of the cultural or subcultural group to which he belongs. He brings with him the apprehensions of his cultural group and the methods of coping that that group has developed. But when the cultural specificity of behavior is not recognized, it may be viewed as symptomatic of pathology. Caseworkers know how to explain marital interactional difficulties when they are derived from inappropriate symbolic meanings each partner has given the other. For example, a wife should not see her husband as a father to her, a husband should not see his wife as a mother to him, and neither parent should see his children as his siblings. Other dynamics, however, may also be at work. For example, the congenitally induced activity pattern of a child may be so different from that of his mother that their interactions become a permanent reproach to each other; an active child disturbs a placid mother, and a placid child is an irritant to an active mother.

Many persons build up a considerable amount of internal disaffection because their self-images are based on antiquated models. If a woman goes through life assessing her behavior against the ideals of behavior that were appropriate for her mother or grandmother, she will surely reach the point of disliking herself. The same holds true for a man, in relation to his father or grandfather. Preoccupation with emulating the past is particularly maladaptive in our society because that society is changing so rapidly that the

99

past can never prepare a person adequately for either the present or the future. And once a person dislikes himself, the road to disliking others is easy to travel.

It is important for the caseworker to become aware of the impact of past cultural experience on family life if he is to understand variations in family dynamics from one population subgroup to another. Irish-American and Jewish-American family life will be given special attention in this presentation. The functions such families serve for their members, the historical destinies that have shaped these functional arrangements, and the maladaptive consequences for people living in a culture dominated by the values and experiences of white Protestant middle-class families have to be considered in establishing a relationship with Irish-American and Jewish-American clients and in setting family treatment goals.

THE IRISH FAMILY: A PATRIARCHAL SYSTEM

When one tries to understand family dynamics, one usually starts at the point at which two young people marry. Understanding an Irish family, however, requires starting at an earlier point. Furthermore, a distinction should be made between an Irish family that has stayed in Ireland and an Irish family that has emigrated to the United States. The reason for such an extension backward in time and a distinction in terms of locale lies in the impact of the essential poverty of Ireland and the strong expression of patriarchal prerogatives that characterizes the Irish family in Ireland. Ireland is essentially a country of small farms. These farms, through subdivision, have now reached the minimum size at which they can maintain a viable agrarian operation. An Irish farmer cannot look forward to having his farm divided among his children after his retirement or death. And he is too poor to be able to provide a dowry for more than one daughter. His problem becomes, therefore, that of selecting one son as his successor in ownership of the farm and one daughter as the recipient of the dowry. His religion prevents him from practicing birth control, and, as a farmer, he welcomes children as the least expensive farm workers he can get.

The Irish family, therefore, is a family rich in children of whom only two will derive economic benefit from the earning and ownership power of their parents. Since there is no established law of succession, the parents are faced with making choices, and they postpone making these choices for a number of reasons. Undoubtedly they want to retain as long as possible their own management of the farm and also the power represented by the funds set aside for the dowry. An equally strong reason for postponement is their reluctance to hurt the children who will not be selected. As a result, marriages in Ireland are long postponed and the proportion of the population that never marries is larger than in other countries.

After the successor has been selected and a husband for the chosen daughter has been found, the other children must leave the farm. They do so in financial straits and with the emotional burden of having been rejected; they must "travel," as the saying goes. In large numbers these rejected sons and daughters have found their way to the United States. Here they have had the opportunity of making good economically, but they have been delayed in beginning the struggle for success and may be burdened with feelings of defeat. It is easy to understand that some of these Irish newcomers have undergone strong compensatory experiences in which they have proved to the world and to themselves that their father probably made the wrong choices. Others, finding life here difficult, have received the painful confirmation that their father's rejection was probably justified by their own failings.

With such a background, the Irish-American family is likely to show strong ties among brothers and sisters. There is a sense of unity of destiny that makes one son—often when he cannot afford to do so—send for his brothers and sisters or help strangers from his country or region. The collateral relative of an Irish client is likely to be of great importance in his family life. Moreover, the Irish client is likely to have great ambivalence in regard to the past; having been rejected, he is likely to harbor negative feelings toward parents and authority figures. At the same time, he has been caught directly or indirectly in dependency strivings, self-doubt, and various forms of regression. For the successful Irishman the problem has been solved. But for the unsuccessful Irish family, such as is encountered in the caseload of a family agency, the family goal of overcoming the history of parental rejection by success in the here and now has not been achieved.

Connected with the problem of family goals is the problem of family ways. Irish people have learned on the farm, and particularly on the non-mechanized farm, that there is men's work and women's work; there is no interchange of functions. The man works in the fields, garden, and barn; the woman works in the house. The same division of labor is frequently maintained by Irish people in this country. The suggestion, for instance, that the woman take a job and the man mind the house and the children if he is unemployed or that the husband nurse his wife when she is ill encounter tradition-based resistance in the client of Irish descent. Probably the man is more resistant than the woman because he rightly suspects that the accustomed patriarchal arrangements cannot be maintained when functions are interchangeable.

The caseworker, therefore, must be aware of the fact that the Irish client is a person whose past experience has been one of exploitation and rejection, whose problem for the future is to overcome the feeling of inferiority and injustice generated in him, and whose family ways—learned in a tradition of Catholicism and an agrarian economy—are patriarchal and resistive to the equalitarian ideal of the American family. Though the Irish-American family's goal is to overcome the emotional insults of the past, the caseworker is unlikely to encounter agreement between husband and wife in relation to family ways of doing things. As far as personal resources and personal obligations are concerned, the family maintains strong collateral ties in which brothers and sisters play a role rarely encountered in a white middle-class Protestant family life.

THE JEWISH FAMILY: A MATRIARCHAL SYSTEM

One of the paradoxes of modern history is that the United States is probably the only nation in which the pattern of Russian-Jewish family life is still maintained, or, at least, still traceable in the ongoing transition to other family patterns. In all probability it is revolutions and wars that have extinguished the pattern in Russia, Poland, and Central Europe. And experimentation with new social arrangements has made it difficult for it to be transplanted or to regenerate itself in Israel.

In historical perspective the Jewish family in Russia is an urban family dispersed in an ocean of agrarian life and a part of a persecuted minority in an ocean of gentiles; it must maintain itself in readiness for crisis. The husband, in making a living, must deal permanently with members of a latently or openly hostile majority; he can maintain himself only by suppression of any aggressiveness that his continuing encounter with hostility and contempt may produce. The wife must be ready to assume emergency functions in the face of persecution, to be the breadwinner as well as the child-rearer, and to maintain the children's feeling of family and group identity. Only in scholarship and religious service does the Jewish husband experience superiority or satisfaction in his striving for self-respect. But even then reality may trip him up; frequently his wife is the breadwinner who makes possible his dedication to scholarship—and where there is economic power, there is social power. In essence, what the Jewish husband cannot be for his wife is a protector in the struggles of living, a warrior on whom she can rely to defeat her enemies, or a symbol of authority based on the reality of power. Consequently, the Jewish woman, consciously or unconsciously, is disappointed in her husband and projects her hopes and wishes for a protector and a comforting masculine figure onto her son. The Jewish husband, having to live with hostility outside his home and a disappointed woman in his home, turns to his daughter for the emotional gratification he needs from a feminine source.

Because of the continuation of unfavorable social and economic conditions, expectations of sounder masculinity in the son and sounder femininity in the daughter are not likely to be fulfilled. The son becomes a relatively weak male; the daughter becomes a disappointed woman and frequently a domineering one. In spite of these negative elements, Jewish family members share a sense of destiny; they share their suffering and have the common goal of overcoming their destiny. Whereas the Irish-American is concerned with undoing the past, the Russian-Jewish family in the United States is concerned with undoing the present. Centuries of persecution and genocide have left on the Jewish family a mark of anxiety about the present, and the family's dominant goal is to make the present safer than it appears to be.

Jewish family ways, strangely enough, are not so different from American white Protestant family ways as are Irish-American family ways. The separation of work from the home, the urbanization of life, and the increasing acceptance of women in positions of employment at most levels of our corporate life have made the roles of husband and wife somewhat similar for both white Protestant and Jewish families. Of course, there is a tremendous difference between the white Protestant middle-class family's history of security and the Jewish family's history of anxiety. However, the interchangeability of the roles of husband and wife has become the pattern in both groups. Moreover, anxiety about the present is beginning to appear in the white Protestant middle-class family as it faces the fact that it has little chance of progressing beyond what it has already achieved. While the experience of minority status vis-à-vis the gentile is still the major source of anxiety for the Jewish family, the white Protestant middle-class family has become a victim of anxiety about maintaining a standard of living and about the diminishing opportunities for advancement in a society in which there is increasingly less room at the top and no new frontier to go to.

TODAY'S REALITY

Is either the patriarchal model of the Irish-American family or the matriarchal model of the Jewish-American family appropriate to the reality of today?

In almost all families the caseworker sees, the husband is found to be weak and passive and the woman to be powerful, active, and aggressive. A consulting psychiatrist is likely to suggest that the husband should become stronger and the wife weaker; but they never do. It can be argued that, under modern living conditions, the problems of masculinity and femininity in family life cannot be solved on the basis of such antiquated models as have been described. First of all, the American standard of living makes it impossible for most women to devote themselves exclusively to the home. The husband and wife must pool earnings if their standard of living is to be maintained. There is also the problem of security for old age, since filial support of aged parents is disappearing from our mores as an obligation. Equally significant is the fact that women and men cannot be educated in an identical manner and then be expected to lead different kinds of lives and make different uses of their education. Moreover, one cannot embrace an ideal of sexual equality and also support the desirability of male superiority. Our ideology does not permit it; the educational system does not permit it; and the economic system does not permit it. But we have not learned to live comfortably with our new institutions, because human beings do not really want equality.

We must begin to think about reformulating behavioral expectations so that they reflect today's demands in regard to masculinity and femininity. The modern American family and the modern cultural value system require that we delineate new ways in which men and women should behave toward each other in order to gratify the need for inequality. Inequality can lead to superiority for each of the marriage partners, but it will not be the same kind of superiority. What is really at issue is the redistribution of the marital partners' superiority experiences. Such a redistribution might have an excellent effect on children in that it should liberate them from exploitation as substitutes. And essential equity in human affairs demands that one should not be called upon emotionally to do another person's job: children should not be called upon to compensate fathers and mothers for their marital disappointments.

In any casework attempt to help marriage partners redistribute superiority between themselves, the concept of individuality is helpful. It can be a valid basis for helping clients learn how to help each other toward a fulfillment of personal identity. The individuality of the one must strengthen the individuality of the other.

The principle of complementarity is also useful. A strong male does indeed make a woman assert her femininity; an authoritarian personality brings out the submissiveness in another; and pronounced youth brings out pronounced maturity. What is needed most in every marriage today is liberation from ambivalence about wanting to be both strong and weak and from wanting to receive gratification from being both. For example, women want to be earners, they want to be strong, they want to vote, and they also want to be feminine and dependent at home. We have not yet learned to look upon the home as a refuge for regression, a refuge from the equality society seems to expect. Nor is there anything absurd about a home in which power is given to a man who, in his work situation, is constantly beset by supervisors on whose approval he is dependent. And it should not be frightening to think that a female director of casework or a woman professor of anatomy may be able to work in her kitchen without calling upon her husband for help. One can shift role and status. And perhaps the family home should be a place where individual differences in terms of strength and weakness are permitted and where the pain of ambivalence about equality can be eased.

Of course, the strength of one marriage partner will be welcome to the other only if it fosters his own value system. If the partners have different goals, growing strength in either or both will only produce more and more conflict.

The problem of masculinity and femininity must also be looked upon in developmental terms. In his lifetime, a male must be permitted to be a boy, a man, and an old man; a woman must be permitted to be a girl, a woman, and an old woman. Apparently, however, neither sex in modern family life is granted these privileges. We are all supposed to be relatively young at any age; women are supposed to combine an appearance of youth with maturity of judgment; and no one is really permitted to grow old. These social attitudes result in our making demands on ourselves that cannot be fulfilled. A healthy family model is one in which family members permit one another to age and even to die; everyone is allowed to grow throughout the full life cycle, not merely to maturity, but to the end of life. If one is able to help another person achieve autonomy, one achieves it oneself.

Dr. Pollak's comments on equality, complementarity, and the affirmation of difference elicited various discussion, and questions were raised. Should one speak of equity rather than equality, since *equity* affirms the existence of difference but allows a common basis in terms of rights? The distinction is an important one to make. One staff member thought it would be helpful to approach the issues raised in terms of mature emotional exchange rather than in terms of sexually predetermined tasks. Human beings are both strong and gentle; men and women can learn when to prevail and when to yield as the need for doing the one or the other varies in accordance with different life stages. For example, a woman who is pregnant or nurturing small children needs special protection and finds it necessary to be yielding. Each life task makes its own particular demands.

It was suggested that one element of maturity is awareness of the temporary nature of attainment and of human needs for periodic rest and relaxation. Each human being needs a chance to grow and change and a chance to remain as he is; the need for change is balanced by the need for sameness. In our society it is extremely difficult to realize one's full potential at each phase of life—particularly in old age—because we do not seem to value true individuation.

After making these general observations, the group turned its attention to Dr. Pollak's comments about Jewish family life in particular. Two questions were raised: (1) Is the historical model of the Jewish family presented by Dr. Pollak valid? (2) Is such a model traceable in the families that come to the agency today?

Staff members found it difficult to identify factors that differentiate the Jewish family from the non-Jewish family in our society. But the suggestion was made that the Jewish mother feels, distinctively, that she must sacrifice herself for her children—and the opinion was expressed that she is inclined to "present her bill" in the form of an unbreakable tie. Some participants argued that similar attitudes are also to be found in Irish and Mennonite mothers—the difference being that the Jewish mother verbalizes such attitudes and feelings more freely and thereby places her children, particularly her son, under strong obligation. It was suggested that the Jewish male's feelings of anger and guilt toward the female may stem from a feeling that he has been given more than he has been able to return.

Question was raised about what happens to a family when the marital relationship becomes strained, and various ideas were put forward. A non-Jewish father, it was suggested, is more likely than a Jewish one to leave his wife for a next-door neighbor with whom he has "fallen in love." In the Jewish family, there is greater likelihood that the husband and wife will sustain the marital tie, even though hostile toward one another, keeping the family together for the children's sake. Jewish couples have been known to maintain twenty or thirty years of silence and then separate in old age. It was suggested that the Jewish stress on maintaining marriages might stem from a historic need for self-maintenance in a hostile environment. By and large, fewer instances of violent "acting out" have been found in the Jewish group than in the general population, even though in recent years there seems to have been an increase.

Participants endeavored to identify specifically Jewish values passed on from the older to the younger generation but found it difficult to do so. Doing good deeds, taking care of those in need, and getting along with one's neighbors reflect, of course, common Judeo-Christian values. Rage and hatred are not accepted, but denied and suppressed in most families. These emotions are tolerated in the Jewish family even less than is usual, because Jewish children are expected to show respect for their elders regardless of how they feel toward them. The concept of filial duty has been preserved in many Jewish families and is found with particular frequency among aged clients. This attitude, however, may be European rather than specifically Jewish; in most European countries children are expected to assume responsibility for their parents. In the Jewish tradition, all the children share responsibility for their elders.

In summing up, it was said that the Jewish family in present-day America is assimilated by and large but that some beliefs and traditions of the past and some specific values can still be isolated. Discussants, understandably, had different points of view; some thought there were significant differences between Jewish- and non-Jewish-American families.

The concept of superiority in the family set forth by Dr. Pollak was considered a key issue. Is it really necessary that one partner establish his superiority? Does this alone allow for real complementarity? If there are two equals, particularly strong equals, what happens to the dependence-independence balance? Rilke's definition of a love relationship was cited: He sees two lovers as "two solitudes who greet and protect each other." It was pointed out that the equality this definition assumes demands great maturity and sophistication. If one pleads for the establishment of superiority in a marital relationship, on the other hand, does it have to be absolute? Can it not be differentially intellectual, emotional, and educational? One spouse may be superior in one area and the other in another. In this regard it is important to know how common decisions are made: Is there room for compromise? Is each spouse concerned for the welfare of the other? Decision-making relates both to the goals of the marriage and the partners' concepts of their roles. How does a wife see herself in relation to her husband, and vice versa? It requires true maturity on the part of each partner if each is to accept the need for yielding to the other and still retain a sense of individual identity.

The point was made that caseworkers have to assess the psychosexual development of their clients and, since many have only a hazy concept of their roles in marriage, help them become more mature as men and women. Sometimes they are made uneasy and anxious by the thought that they should strive for equality; they may find it much more comfortable to accept superiority in one partner. Only the truly mature person, who has experienced his own identity, can accept the concept of equality.

5

FAMILY GROUP DIAGNOSIS
AND TREATMENT

Gertrude Einstein

Instead of making a formal presentation of the theory of family group diagnosis and treatment, Dr. Gabriel d'Amato, the agency's psychiatric consultant, presented a case example of family group treatment. Staff discussion was based on the case he presented, and certain principles of family interviewing were identified.

Particularly in family treatment, diagnosis and treatment are inseparable. The counselor's therapeutic intent should be conveyed to family members early in the contact. Simultaneously, the counselor must try to learn enough about the family's history and its life style so that he can understand the dynamics that are operating. The purpose of conjoint family interviewing is to free a family from fixed patterns of communication and of relationship that are destructive and to provide family members an opportunity to develop healthier, more constructive patterns. Through his observation of the functioning of the family as a unit, the helper, or therapist, is enabled to define the family's problems, evaluate its strengths and weaknesses, decide upon appropriate treatment goals, and gear his interventive efforts toward the strengthening of the family's own problem-solving and decision-making capacities.

The worker's close observation of verbal and nonverbal communications between family members and his ability to probe the meaning of these verbal and nonverbal messages are essential to his understanding of family interaction. He must also assess family members' expectations of one another, the alliances they form, and the homeostatic mechanisms that are used to maintain accustomed patterns, as against their willingness and

109

ability to respond to new situations and different challenges. The worker gears his intervention toward helping the family achieve a new balance, a more flexible response than before to new situations and demands, and more realistic mutual expectations.

It is vital for the worker, in treating the family unit, to view the family as a social system. He must understand the purpose served by the symptoms displayed, what roles each family member carries, how the family tries to solve its problems, and which family patterns have become fixed. In family diagnosis and treatment, focus shifts from individuals to the family unit as a whole—and if the therapist makes the mistake of concentrating on the pathology of one family member, his treatment may be ineffective. To be responsive to the many unexpected elements that can emerge in family treatment, the therapist has to be flexible and open-minded. He must maintain a constant responsiveness to the new and unanticipated, which may be acted out in the here and now, and his response must be immediate and yet purposeful. Working with the whole family makes great demands on the worker's skill.

In the ensuing discussion numerous questions were raised concerning agency practice with respect to family treatment. At what point in a case should family interviews be scheduled? Reference was made to the fact that a waiting list for service makes it imperative to determine next steps in treatment during the initial contact. For example, should immediate help be offered? Should the client be referred to another resource? Or should the case be put on the waiting list? There was general agreement that a family interview often results in a quicker and more accurate diagnosis than do several individual interviews, since it provides a framework within which customary family functioning is brought into the open for all to see: distortions, projections, contradictions, lack of communication, and improper communication all come to light, as do family strengths, the members' readiness to offer each other support, and the family's general coping capacity. Consequently, it is a sound procedure to hold a family interview at an early point in the intake process.

The individual worker's skill and his comfort with the family interview are important factors in deciding if and when to schedule such an interview. Equally important is the family's readiness to begin as a family, the members' ability to see the presented problem as one that involves all, or most, of them.

Some complex technical issues were discussed. What constitutes a family unit? Should all members of the family be involved, even very young children? It was noted that some therapists hold that at least those family members living in one household should be included in the early interviews, since it may be important to observe parental attitudes not only toward older children but also toward an infant. Moreover, an absent family member may, consciously or unconsciously, sabotage treatment.[1] Some therapists,

---

[1] See John C. Sonne, Ross V. Speck, and Jerome E. Jungreis, "The Absent-Member Maneuver as a Family Resistance," in Alfred S. Friedman and others, *Psychotherapy for the Whole Family,* Springer Publishing Co., New York 1965, pp. 263–74.

on the other hand, think that interviewing arrangements must be flexible, since not all family members can tolerate consistent involvement, whether for psychological or for practical reasons. When services are provided for older persons, members of the immediate family can sometimes be interviewed together with interested persons outside the family, when the latter play a key role in planning for the older person. This is a special use of the family group interview.

Those counselors who had used the family group modality agreed that in family group treatment there usually is some one family member who represents an element of strength in the family, who presses for continuation of treatment, and who carries the other members along with him. Frequently this person is the mother, although during the course of treatment another member may assume the progressive role. Similarly, one family member may act out the family's resistances and find ways of interfering with the treatment plan.

An important task of the therapist in a family interview is to ease the pressure on whichever family member has been "put on the spot" by the others. In successive interviews, the same person may not always be the target of assault, even though many families have a chosen scapegoat. The family gestalt is fluid and alliances shift from interview to interview; the therapist must be constantly alert to multiple exchanges at various psychological levels. A cotherapist, though adding some new complications, can be a great asset in family interviews. Ideally, the two therapists should be a man and a woman so that an identification model is provided for both male and female family members. Cotherapists can be of the same sex, however, without jeopardy to the family. The functioning of cotherapists, including the matter of competition and other attitudes and feelings, requires much more experimentation and study. Work with the whole family group opens up new vistas to those who undertake it. But it should be done only when specific consultation or supervision is available.

THE BROWNSTEIN CASE*

Mr. Brownstein, aged 53 years, salesman
Mrs. Brownstein, aged 45 years, stenographer
David, aged 14 years, student
Joseph, aged 11 years, student

The following case is presented from three perspectives: the summary prepared for psychiatric consultation, excerpts from the case record, and an analysis of family relationships.

SUMMARY PREPARED FOR PSYCHIATRIC CONSULTATION, JUNE 6

The objectives of consultation are the following: (1) to consider whether counseling or psychiatric treatment is the treatment of choice for David; (2) to consider whether David is accessible for help in his present frame of mind; and (3) to help formulate appropriate goals if a continued relationship is indicated, taking into account David's pathological avoidance of interpersonal relations.

The Client's Statement of the Current Problem

Mrs. B telephoned the agency, having been referred by the rabbi of her synagogue. She stated that the problem concerned David, who was not doing well at school and was a problem "on the street." The problem had come to a head when David had been found to have in his possession some papers belonging to the school and had been suspended as a result. Mrs. B had discussed the problem with David, and he had decided he should get some "help." Mrs. B had telephoned the rabbi, who had referred her to the agency.

Previous Contact

Five years earlier, Mrs. B had telephoned the agency at the suggestion of the school counselor. David had been doing poor work and had not seemed able to apply himself. When offered an appointment to determine whether the agency or a child guidance clinic would be the more appropriate source of help for David, Mrs. B had withdrawn, saying she would discuss the problem with the school counselor. The case was later closed since there was no further contact.

Contact with School Counselor

The school counselor reported that David's main problem at school is that he does not apply himself. He displays no interest in school and, from

* Submitted by Gertrude Einstein. Beginning interviews held by Hugh Rosen.

every indication, does not even try to do satisfactory work. Despite this, aptitude tests show that David has above-average ability. Recently he has been getting into "bits of difficulty" because of his behavior. He has resorted to lying to get out of trouble. The school counselor said that David's face is consistently expressionless. An entry put in David's school record five years earlier stated that he was bored, made no effort, was failing, and never did homework.

David's report cards from the first grade onward reveal a fairly consistent pattern of behavior. He is characterized by his teachers as a shy, unhappy boy who is inattentive and teases his schoolmates a great deal. He is unexpressive but easily moved to tears. There is general agreement that David has a capacity for better work than he is doing but seems to be unmotivated.

Contact with B'nai B'rith Vocational Service

David was tested by the B'nai B'rith Vocational Service fourteen months ago. It was felt that he had superior potential, although his verbal capacity was not well-developed. In mathematics his score placed him in the top 25 per cent of thirteen-year-old youngsters. His vocabulary was advanced, on a par with children in the ninth grade. His verbal ability was average but his reading level was low. Mrs. B was described as being "too busy." She was said to be too indulgent in some ways and too limiting in others. She customarily stood over David as he did his homework.

It was learned that Mr. B was suffering from a chronic illness contracted as a result of a war injury. David had been told that the illness was caused largely by Mr. B's concern for him, which had probably generated guilt feelings in him.

The overriding conclusion drawn from testing was that David's inability to utilize his potential was primarily the result of an emotional disturbance. The recommendation was made that Mrs. B apply to the agency for help, but there was no record that she had done so. In a recent interview Mrs. B denied having been advised to seek help from the agency at the time of the tests.

Previous Psychiatric Treatment

Five years ago Mr. and Mrs. B and David were in therapy at a psychological testing clinic, now out of existence. Each of the three had a different therapist and continued for about eight months. Treatment was terminated for all when David's therapist decided that the boy lacked sufficient motivation to continue.

Mrs. B reported during her first interview at the agency that she had become aware of the role she played in David's emotional disturbance during her period of therapy. It seemed, however, that she emphasized this point excessively as if to ward off any anticipated "accusations." The same approach revealed itself later as a pattern.

David's Agency Experience

David has been interviewed only once. He spoke rather inarticulately and often inaudibly. He rarely gazed directly at the counselor; most of the time he stared at the floor. He was angry and hostile about being at the office but denied it when the possibility was suggested to him. He did say, however, that he had been "blackmailed" into coming; he said that several weeks earlier his mother had confiscated some school forms that were illicitly in his possession and had threatened to turn them over to the principal unless David agreed to come to the agency.

David was unable to admit he had any problem in relation to his parents. He perceived his problem exclusively as having to do with school. He found he was unable to study or even grasp material when he did apply himself. David spoke of having had therapy and said it had not been helpful to him; he said the therapist just kept asking what his problems were. David asked whether he would have to come to the agency during the summer; he did not feel he should because his problem related only to school and he would not attend classes during the summer. David was very manipulative in trying to get future appointments that would conflict with his school schedule, so that he could leave school early. He accepted the worker's refusal in silence.

Mr. and Mrs. B's Agency Experience

Mr. and Mrs. B have been seen in two joint interviews. Mrs. B has also been seen in two individual interviews. When they were seen together, Mrs. B proved to be the more verbal and dominant although Mr. B made a greater effort to express himself in the second joint interview.

Mr. B, although thin and slight of build, has an essentially masculine, and even somewhat rough, appearance. When attempting to express himself, he moves at a slow pace because of what appears to be a difficulty in conceptualizing and an impoverished vocabulary. His manner, in this regard, is suggestive of David's but not so extreme. Mr. B seems genuinely concerned about David's problem but singularly lacking in any appreciation of the role that emotional disturbance can play in such a conflict as David's. Mr. B tends simply to perceive David as a lazy boy whose apathy can be remedied by the proper exercise of will power. Consequently, he has little patience in dealing with David. On a few occasions Mr. B has beaten David severely. Besides being ineffective, the beatings usually make Mr. B feel worse than David; Mr. B suffers from ulcers, and such episodes aggravate them considerably.

It seems that Mr. and Mrs. B are inclined to use disciplinary measures that are basically self-defeating. For example, they lament the fact that David does not socialize and yet punish him by restricting him to the house for weeks at a time; at other times they punish him by discontinuing his allowance.

Mrs. B is an aggressive, manipulating woman who attempts to disguise these tendencies by assuming an amiable manner. She persists in formulating specific questions that she hurls at the counselor, often in an attacking manner. These questions are ostensibly designed to elicit "enlightenment" that will enable her to resolve David's problem. Although she has been repeatedly told that the resolution of the problem cannot be achieved in this way, she continues to pursue a direct line of questioning, apparently in an effort to ward off a more immediate engagement of herself. From the first Mrs. B has attempted to manipulate the counselor into allowing her to bring David to the office. She stresses David's eagerness to come to the agency and urges that advantage be taken of his readiness. She has even quoted him as having said: "Mommy, when will they call me in, when I'm already crazy?" David's tale of "blackmail" suggested that Mrs. B was grossly distorting the true situation. Her manipulativeness and lack of fidelity to truth are significantly revealing of her pattern of relating to people.

In an early interview Mrs. B had maintained that her marriage was a sound one. In a later interview, however, she reported that she had had a most distressful argument with Mr. B, which had made her doubt that she had *ever* really had a good relationship with him. She was visibly upset and said it would eventually be necessary for her to reveal the subject of the argument; she could not do so immediately.

During the discussion of David's prospective first interview, Mrs. B showed considerable anxiety about how he would come to the agency. She did not appear to be willing to let him come alone and wanted to accompany him. She projected her anxiety onto David, saying that traveling alone on an unfamiliar route would be upsetting for him. She had her way: David's father drove him to the agency and returned to take him home. David himself displayed no special concern about traveling alone. Mrs. B has said that she fears the anxiety she and Mr. B feel about David is being communicated to him and that it is detrimental to their relationship with him.

David's Pathology

David's principal behavioral problems are stealing and lying. The stealing is usually confined to taking money from his parents, although not exclusively. Recently he was suspended briefly from school for having taken some forms from a teacher's desk. He was first known to steal shortly after starting school, at which time he took something belonging to a little girl. Throughout the years his stealing has become progressively worse.

As David grew up, he made friends but always seemed to gravitate toward boys who got into trouble. He generally associated with boys with aggressive personalities, even though he was unable to handle them. Often the boys beat him up, and he refused to defend himself. When urged to fight back, he replied that doing so would only cause more boys to assault him.

During the past several months David has withdrawn more and more and rarely goes out. He has no friends at all now and stays at home, watching television most of the time. He never verbalizes his feelings and is generally expressionless.

Some of Mrs. B's questions have made it clear that she suspects that David's problem may involve mental illness. More than once she has expressed concern about the possibility of David's needing psychiatric treatment, and she once spoke of having read a description of schizophrenia that reminded her and Mr. B of David. Mrs. B has not yet fully revealed the depth of her fears about David's mental health; she tends to couch her questions and discussion in objective terms, attempting to suggest that she is pursuing the matter out of curiosity.

Background

As a baby and young child David was well-behaved. Mrs. B described him as a "little man." When he was two, neighbors sought opportunities to watch and admire him. He was three-and-a-half years of age when his brother, Joseph, was born. The following month David began to wet his bed, which he continued to do until he was eleven years of age. David often teased his brother; recently, however, Joseph has been teasing David.

Casework Evaluation

David's problem is a complex one. He seeks out punishment quite actively. Accustomed to misunderstanding, attack, and ineffectual punitive measures on his parents' part, David, until recently when he has become seclusive, has sought out peers who are aggressive and difficult for him to relate to and who have even beaten him. He has developed a passive-aggressive pattern of relating. Having been subjected to Mrs. B's manipulating control, he has attempted to wield this same kind of control over others but has had less success. In his relationship with Mrs. B, David has encountered emotional dishonesty, excessive anxiety about his physical well-being, and a destructively controlling interference, all of which have contributed toward generating in him a basic fear and distrust of his total environment. Mrs. B's disproportionate anxiety about David conceals an underlying rejection of the boy, of which he is not completely unaware.

Because both Mr. B and David have been subject to Mrs. B's domination and because David's difficulty in verbal expression is so suggestive of his father's, it is probable that Mr. B's attitude toward David represents self-condemnation and that he projects onto David a hatred of himself.

Goals for the B Family

David needs an experience in which he can express himself freely and without fear of rejection to someone in whom he senses he can place trust. It will have to be discovered whether he will let himself use such an opportunity.

Mrs. B should be encouraged to examine her real feelings toward David, which would involve coming to terms with the projection of her own anxieties onto him. She needs help in differentiating between her feelings toward her husband and those toward her elder son.

Mr. B needs to understand that David is emotionally disturbed, not just "lazy." If he can be helped to value himself more, he may become able to give a different "message" to David.

Questions

Following are the counselor's questions for the psychiatric consultant:

1. Is psychiatric treatment rather than casework the preferred treatment for David?

2. What is the meaning of his pathological behavior, particularly his tendency to withdraw from relationships, while his anxiety results in his acting out in some situations?

116

3. Are Mrs. B's feelings toward her husband and her son so intimately bound up together that she has a greatly distorted picture of David?

4. Would it be too threatening to Mrs. B to work on her insight into her projection of anxiety onto David, to recognize her own anxiety for what it is and possibly even to learn that she has been rejecting him all this time?

5. It is possible that Mr. B has been engaging in self-condemnation because of the thwarting role he has played in David's growth, in view of the similarity between the two. In the light of his past history, what is the prognosis for Mr. B?

6. Is there any indication that family therapy might be the treatment of choice, and what resources exist for such therapy?

Counselor's Summary of Psychiatric Consultation

In interpreting David's situation, the psychiatric consultant noted that both parents are reflected in his make-up. It is likely that David's acting-out has value for his mother in that it provides her a measure of satisfaction for her own unconscious delinquent impulses. The consultant suggested a diagnosis of passive-aggressive character disorder or of borderline schizophrenia, pointing out that the symptoms of the two categories of disturbance are not mutually exclusive. It appears that David's personality is undergoing a transformation toward a schizophrenic orientation, as manifested in his expressionless quality and increasing social withdrawal. Given this situation, a discontinuance of stealing by David could be an alarming sign, suggesting further that he is slipping into schizophrenia.

The consultant observed that David is not likely to change for the better until his parents evidence a willingness to do so as well and recommended either a series of family group interviews or institutional placement and treatment of David. Discussion centered principally around the former recommendation, and it was agreed that a series of from four to six interviews would be conducted with the family as a group. On the basis of the interviews, which would be exploratory, the next step would be determined, possibly referral to a psychiatric clinic for family therapy. Finally, close collaboration between the family counselor and the consultant was advised.

The case was transferred to a worker who was ready to offer family interviews.

EXCERPTS FROM THE CASE RECORD

First Family Interview, September 25

The difference between Mr. and Mrs. B is striking. Mr. B gives the impression of being a workman. He has irregular, not very attractive features; his best features are his blue eyes and his direct and steady gaze. Mrs. B gives the impression of being middle class. She is fairly attractive, without being pretty. She is clearly the strongest person in the family. David, who has regular features and is tall for his age, is by far the nicest-looking member of the family; with downcast eyes, he was withdrawn, at least at the beginning of the interview. Joseph, much less good-looking, has a round, placid face and wears glasses; in contrast to David he gave no evidence of anxiety. Joseph took the chair next to his mother; David seemed hesitant, waiting until everyone else was seated, and then sat between Joseph and his father.

The interview started with my stressing the exploratory nature of the meetings and the hope that the family members would contribute to finding ways they could be happier as a family. In order to have answers, I said, understanding was needed.

The beginning of the interview was focused completely on David, as Mr. B complained about his being "disrespectful" and not doing what he was told. When invited to be more specific, Mr. B spoke about David's not coming home when he was supposed to and having to be sent after. Immediately Mr. and Mrs. B disagreed about the underlying facts. The children were listening intently but not participating. Joseph looked at me. David, with his eyes still downcast, looked me over furtively. Again there was a discrepancy between Mr. and Mrs. B's views of the situation in the discussion about David's friends. Mrs. B complained that David did not bring them home; Mr. B said that he did not want them in the house because they were "not nice boys." The story of David's having been beaten up by these boys was alluded to. David attempted several times to say something, but he could not assert himself. Later he was more responsive when I tried to draw him into more neutral discussions, and his mother immediately complained that he was not courteous to me. She said, accurately, that he was angry; I asked whether his slightly discourteous manner might not be an expression of anger to which he was entitled. Then Mrs. B discussed at length David's general failure to show anger, and said she sometimes goads him because she wishes he would show what he feels. I pointed out that when David had just shown anger, Mrs. B had not seemed to like it. She said she wanted David to express his anger more directly, being able to remember only one outburst of temper on David's part when he was about two years old and none since. I said I wondered how other people in the family experienced and handled anger. Joseph yells, slams the door, and runs to his room. Mrs. B did not reply specifically, adding that she is sometimes not sure how she feels, and thinks David may sometimes also be uncertain how he feels. When Mrs. B complained about David's lack of social life and his not going with the "right" boys, I redirected the discussion away from David and to the B's social life in general. Mr. B, who has had very little education and wants more for his sons, has found bowling at a club where men congregate to be his best outlet. The family tried bowling together, but it did not work out. The onus for the failure of the family venture was put on David, but it was clear from further discussion that there were other reasons, too. Mr. B mentioned that his low earnings—in spite of long, hard hours of work—also affected the family's social life. Referring to his previously adequate income, Mr. B expressed some feeling about Mrs. B's having to work. She, too, while acknowledging she enjoys her work as a stenographer, made it clear that she only works because of family needs. David became more relaxed and freer as the focus of discussion was shifted away from him. I pointed out that the family obviously has problems other than David,

118

namely, financial and social problems. Mrs. B then asked David outright whether he thought she had been "more crabby" since the family's financial difficulties began. David said, "Yes," adding that his father was "just the same." Joseph, who was also asked by his mother, immediately said, "No." In discussion about David's anger, there was again a difference between the parents' views: Mr. B has seen David angry, and Mrs. B has not. Again taking the onus off David, I asked about allowances for the children, and how the B's had had to make adjustments in what they could allow the children financially. Both children get $1.00 a week. Mrs. B explained defensively that Joseph spends 50 cents of his allowance on going to the movies nearly every week and that she wants him to save the 50 cents when he does not go to the movies. David, however, does not go to the movies. I asked whether, not going to the movies, David was free to save the 50-cent admission fee or spend it for something else. David then spoke up, saying that a dollar does not take a fellow very far. At one other point he had also spoken up, saying that the boy his father had wanted to keep him away from was not really the one who had beaten him up. From David's behavior over-all, it can be seen that he has given up asserting himself and even trying to make himself understood; there are clear signs of progressive withdrawal.

In terms of family dynamics, Mrs. B is the key person, superior to Mr. B in social class and intelligence, and she makes her superiority clear to him. Selecting Mr. B as a partner may have constituted an attempt to buttress her unsure feelings about her own value. She mentioned at one time that her mother "always knew what was the right thing to do"; she maintained the "always" against challenge, while she implied that she herself does not have much wisdom. The complying child, Joseph, does not put her to the test as David does, and he is "her boy." He is also accepted by his father. David has been put into a double bind: at the same time, his mother says to him, "Show me your feelings" and "I won't tolerate what you show me." Mr. B takes all his cues from his wife and, afraid of her sugar-coated hostility, retreats before she can attack.

In this family constellation, David is terribly alone. His relationship to Joseph does not seem to be too bad, but it cannot be really positive because of Joseph's being the good, accepted child.

Telephone Contact, October 2

Mrs. B telephoned. David and Joseph are sick—David with a fever and Joseph with an earache. She asked whether she and Mr. B should keep the family appointment alone. I recommended that they not do so on the ground that the children might feel excluded. Mrs. B then told me that David wanted to come and that the entire family would keep the scheduled appointment if David's temperature went down. Mrs. B said she would call me later in the day.

Second Family Interview, October 2

The family came at the scheduled time. In this interview, family relationships were further explored. Mr. B. holds in his anger against his wife but

119

not against David. Sometimes when he comes home irritated with his customers, David "lights the match," touching off his anger. At times he is angry with himself and goes to his room and berates himself. David does not like to go with his father and work for him on the truck because of the tension between them. Mr. B's ulcer operation, which had taken place two years earlier, was mentioned as another reason for tension; subsequently his earnings had declined drastically. The financial restrictions of the family were discussed again. In speaking of former times, Mrs. B mentioned that, in previous therapy sessions, she had discussed with the therapist her standing over David when he had been a little boy and pushing him into doing the things she wanted; she said she was trying hard not to do so any longer. In this connection, we talked about Mrs. B's childhood and her apparent need to make it altogether nice and good in her memory, even though her family had been very poor. I suggested she was perhaps again "in her own family" and wanted to have everything so nice that no one was allowed to say what he really thought, or to be angry. We then discussed David's behavior in the last interview, when he had tried to show a little anger by being somewhat impolite to me, and I pointed out how much Mrs. B had been distressed by his expression of anger. Still, he was angry and his mother knew it. Mrs. B became thoughtful and said that I had "opened a window for her." She displayed more warmth and honesty than she had during the previous interview. She also admitted that every week she asked her husband how much money he had brought home, even though she knew that he could not earn very much beyond his usual limit. Her checking up caused tension between them, which again really had nothing to do with David.

In watching David and Joseph, I noted how they exchanged glances, smiled, and seemed to enjoy it when attention was shifted from them to their parents. The parents mentioned their wish for David to go to college. I questioned whether David could do so because they wanted it or must himself choose or reject going to college. There was some discussion about the suspension of David's allowance and what it means to him. David has not been given an allowance since he started to smoke; nevertheless, his father smokes and once told David that he could smoke if he did so in front of him. Once again the B's were not together and had not made clear to David what was expected of him.

At the end of the interview, I played a short part of the tape of the preceding interview for the family. Mrs. B had an extremely negative reaction to her own voice; she thought it was "bossy," and so did her husband.

The principal focus of this interview, at least for a great part of the time, shifted away from David, and he was considerably more comfortable than he had been during the first interview. Joseph was included at times when problems concerning allowance or bedtime were discussed, and this focus of attention also seemed to relieve David of anxiety, since Joseph did not emerge, as he usually did, as a paragon of virtue.

Third Family Interview, October 8

Seating arrangement: David sat next to Mrs. B; Mr. B sat on the other side of Mrs. B; Joseph sat between Mr. B and me. Relating her question to what she had told me about her family of origin, Mrs. B asked whether I really thought anger was not tolerated in the B family. Subsequently she talked more about her family of origin, and I helped her say that at times she had been very angry with her father; previously she had stressed only her feelings of respect for him. I said I wondered how she had been able to disregard her angry feelings toward her father for so many years. My remark led to a renewal of Mrs. B's earlier comparison of Joseph's ready expression of rage and David's containment of anger. The discrepancy between the parents' verbal and actual reactions again became apparent when the B's said they wished David would, for example, throw an ashtray, as his father had done occasionally. David said his parents would never tolerate such behavior from him. Mrs. B raised the question whether David could not forget that she had pushed him around when he was little, saying she did not wish to do so any longer. I said one does not usually forget such things quickly and speculated that David's uncaring attitude might stem from the time at which he had been little and dependent. David expressed his hopelessness about being heard, saying that no one listened when he tried to say what he wanted. Again there was much talk about an allowance and David's unwillingness to earn extra money by helping his father. Mr. B expressed his real concern for his family, including David, and his frustration at not being able to communicate with David. I likened the family situation to a cold war, suggesting that punishment and hurting seemed to be the only means used of reaching one another. My remark seemed to hit home, particularly for Mrs. B. She claimed that she had stopped sulking, but David contradicted her, saying that she still does so, even though for shorter periods of time. Mr. B referred to his family of origin. His father was authoritarian, and his mother at times took the protective role. He was called upon to fend for himself at an early age, and there is no closeness between him and his siblings. He feels much closer to Mrs. B's family than to his own. Mrs. B spoke of a boy friend she had had before she had met Mr. B and of breaking off her association with him because of her parents' objection that he was not Jewish; she spoke of her difficulty in doing so because of her doubts about her desirability and chances of finding a husband. For the first time I learned that an older sister of Mrs. B's, named Miss F, lived with the B family. Mrs. B supplied this information, adding that she had talked with her sister about the possibility of joining the family interviews and that her sister was willing to do so. I said I regretted not having known the whole situation earlier and thought it best not to alter the composition of the treatment group in midstream. The possible meaning of the presence of an added mother figure in the family was discussed, and the B's provided some information about the situation. The B's feel obligated to the aunt because she has helped them financially in the past. She is a bookkeeper and seems to have strong feelings about being unmarried. Her presence seems to have both good and bad effects on the family. Mrs. B objects when Miss F becomes bossy with the children; David, on the other hand, said that he had gotten along well with his aunt when he spent two weeks with her one summer. Mrs. B responded by saying, "So I am the bossy one."

There was some discussion of the family's further need for help. David, when questioned by his mother, said he would like to have someone to talk to alone, which I thought could be discussed at the next session. David seemed more willing—even though grudgingly—to express himself. From time to time he seemed more relaxed, and twice he and his mother smiled at each other. When Mr. B talked about his family background, Mrs. B turned to David and asked whether he had known about it, to which David replied, "Yes." I emphasized the importance of David's finding out for himself what he wanted—in terms of school and health, for example—and suggested that he might not have done so because it was so easy to react against what his parents suggested. I pointed out that David might find out more easily what he was for if he had nothing to be against. Mrs. B at times spoke rather warmly about David, saying, for instance, that she "respected" him because he was worried about the association of a new friend in the neighborhood with one of the boys he considered undesirable. Even though David has evidently taken little initiative in terms of doing any extra work, Mr. B spoke about a positive change in him, and he obviously had nothing very concrete to complain about. There seems to be a loosening up of the general family atmosphere.

Fourth Family Interview, October 14

Mrs. B started the interview on a very positive note, reporting that David was "wonderful" and that things were very much better. As an illustration, she said that David had helped her clean the windows, which she could not have done alone. David said that his mother had been different, too. When I asked how, he reported that she had not been yelling at him, as she usually did. When I asked about his father, David said he felt no change in him. As an illustration, David reported that if he went in and out of the house frequently, Mr. B became very nervous and was apt to shout at him. We talked a little about adolescent restlessness and the possibility that Mr. B's reaction to David in such a situation arose rather from his own inner tension than from a real objection to David's behavior. There was some discussion of a mutually angry response between Mr. B and David; I suggested that it might have been a demonstration of caring that neither could show as warm feelings.

A large part of the interview was taken up in a discussion of the financial difficulties in the family, which, it became clear, created an enormous amount of tension between Mr. and Mrs. B. Mr. B feels very uncomfortable about not being able to support his family as he feels he should, and Mrs. B is discontent that he does not earn more than he does. She also feels shut out by him. I challenged both and asked whether they could handle their distress differently. I also called their attention to the fact that when talking about it, they had both talked to me rather than to each other. This observation helped them to be more direct. Mr. B, plainly revealing his insecurity, protested that he loved his wife and expressed uncertainty whether she loved him. He said he would like to try to do things differently. There was some discussion of the possibility of Mr. B's consulting an employment agency about moving into a better-paying occupation, but it was clear that Mr. B, accustomed to being self-employed, was not eager to work for a "boss."

122

Also he is not very strong, and his ulcers limit his ability to exert himself.

Mrs. B reported having been very angry with David and David's having begun to be angry in turn; she had curbed him but then realized immediately what she was doing. She has some awareness now that she says one thing and then does another. It was for the first time clearly acknowledged that David has often been the butt of anger not meant for him.

In evaluating the four family interviews held to date, the family members said they thought they had been helped a great deal—except Joseph, who had confided in his mother that he had not been able to keep himself from yawning because he had been so bored. There was a somewhat extensive discussion of possible next steps. Further family interviews or separate interviews, perhaps? David, who formerly wanted separate interviews, is not now sure that he would not prefer to continue family interviews. He could not explain why but accepted my interpretation that his change of mind had come about because so many general family troubles had come out in the interviews. Mrs. B said she thought that, nevertheless, David had troubles of his own, suggesting he might benefit from individual interviews. I agreed, reporting to David that I had talked to the counselor at his former school about his troubles there. David reported that he had so far not had any trouble in his new school. In considering further steps, I suggested that the B's talk about family versus individual interviews and let me know their decision. I believed that separate interviews would be more fruitful and said so. I thought that would enable Mr. and Mrs. B to focus on differences between them, particularly on her feeling that she had married a somewhat ineffective man and his feeling that he was not the good provider he wished to be. I thought David could probably profit from individual interviews focused in some measure on his peer relationships.

I was amazed at the shift in the family after only four interviews. I saw David smile—as if he had begun to move out from under a very heavy burden. The denied tensions between Mr. and Mrs. B were in the open. Joseph was managing quite well by allowing himself to feel whatever he felt, whether angry or bored, and saying so.

Telephone Contact, October 21

Not having heard from the B's, I telephoned and spoke with Mrs. B. She informed me that all had agreed they would prefer a continuation of family interviews, rather than separate counseling for Mr. and Mrs. B and David. I agreed, trusting their wish to involve themselves as a family.

Eighth Family Interview, November 18

The composition of the group was altered by the addition of Mrs. B's sister, Miss F.

Miss F is a tall, heavy-set woman, with dark hair. She is less attractive than Mrs. B, who, though not pretty, has a more graceful figure than her sister. Miss F seemed well informed about the previous family interviews, said she knew "what it was all about," and eventually affirmed that our talking had made sense to her. She talked little, but whenever she did, with a forcefulness similar to Mrs. B's. At one time she accused Mr. B of making mealtime very uncomfortable through his criticism of the children and outbursts at them. She also complained about David's not coming to her for help with his schoolwork when he needed it. Like Mrs. B, she has tried to make David angry and to make him express his anger. There seems to be some competition between the two sisters for the love of the children, and so it may be that Mrs. B's motivation for remonstrating with her sister for "being too much after the children" may be a wish to defeat a rival. David said that he had gotten accustomed to his aunt, that he was able to "discount" her when she was angry or asked him to do things. I cannot remember the words he used, but in explaining his attitude toward his aunt, he made it clear that she was not as emotionally important to him as was his mother.

There was an atmosphere of gloom over the whole family because both boys had brought home very bad report cards. On Joseph's there was a remark to the effect that he did not exert himself and that his work did not come up to average standards. David had been very disappointed by his marks; though he had expected to fail in music, he had not expected to receive low marks in almost every subject, as he had. Joseph handed his report to me, but David did not do so and I did not request it. Mrs. B was filled with anger; saying that the boys would no longer be permitted to look at television, she sounded very punitive and retaliatory. David said, as he had said before, that he could not concentrate, that his mother's anger at him bothered him very much. Mrs. B stressed again David's gifts, which she considered superior to Joseph's, but she stressed them as a basis for complaining and pushing David. Miss F and Mr. B supported Mrs. B, but their attitude was somewhat milder. I tried to explore with the family members how, in a difficult situation like the present one, they related to each other in mounting anger, and I questioned whether they thought such behavior was helpful in changing the situation. Mrs. B said she knew it was not—but she felt angry. She finally gave in to some tears, thus showing unhappiness rather than anger. Miss F tried to make David feel responsible for his mother's unhappiness. As the parents' disappointment in the boys was being discussed, David said that he had experienced some disappointment too, caused by them. His father had promised to take him fishing and had not done so. The fact was revealed that David, as well as his father, did not enjoy fishing, and so it seemed clear that David's disappointment lay in not having found a way of being with his father. In addition, David had been promised new clothing, to be bought on a specific evening, but his parents had not carried out their promise. Mrs. B offered many rationalizations for the failure—and I pointed out again the family's failure to discuss issues and the consequent uncertainty about what should and could be expected.

Reminding the B's that I had expressed some difference with almost every family member at one time or another, I asked whether, at times, I had made them very angry with me. Mrs. B completely denied having ever been angry with me.

I asked permission to call both boys' schools in order to find out what could be done to help them. Neither of the boys objected, nor did the parents. Mrs. B made it clear that she wanted to help Joseph, and that she would supervise his work more closely. She said openly that she did not think she could be truly helpful to David because of getting angry and not having patience with him; David seemed to agree. Both in voice and attitude he evidenced greater depression than he had recently and made no suggestions about improving his school performance. There is no doubt that this boy has unusual difficulties with concentration on any one subject for any length of time. The father's inertia and self-indulgence may have importance as a negative example not only for David but also for the entire family. I left the family members with the question whether they would revert to the angry interaction that had initially sprung from the boys' bad report cards or might perhaps use the circumstance to come closer together in an effort to remedy the situation. I suggested that we discuss the matters of television viewing and recreation at the next interview, since Mrs. B had already understood that taking away every kind of relaxation from the boys certainly would not give them more incentive to learn.

It was planned that Miss F would be with us at the next meeting and would make further appointments with whatever regularity was possible.

Eleventh Family Interview, December 9

Mrs. B stressed in this interview that family sessions had been David's choice, and she said she wondered whether David did not need individual interviews. I myself had planned to suggest individual interviews for David and regretted that Mrs. B had anticipated my move, because David is disinclined to agree to something he knows his mother wants. I said that planning individual interviews for David might be a good idea and that I had thought of it myself. I stressed, however, that I had had the idea not because David was "the problem" but because he did not know what he wanted for himself either currently or in the future and I had thought I might help him with the question alone.

Very early in the interview, Mrs. B encouraged her husband to tell about his anger the previous Sunday morning when he had not found breakfast ready for him and, besides, she had not come downstairs to join him. Anger had built up in Mr. B, and he had not thought to go upstairs to talk to his wife; he would have learned that she was not feeling well. Even so, as against the usual pattern, Mr. B's anger, at least at the beginning, had been clearly directed against his wife, not David. Moreover, Mrs. B had forced a show-down rather than sulk. It did not take long, however, for Mr. B to shift his attention back to David. He had made a rule that, in future, David must come downstairs at ten o'clock on Sundays and join the family for breakfast. I raised the question whether David's doing so would actually be pleasant, since mealtime was not the most congenial time for the B's and also since David seemed to have a strong feeling that there was nothing to get up for. Mrs. B soon took over the discussion, and there followed one of the angriest exchanges that had occurred yet; Mrs. B's rage blazed, and she attacked David particularly for not helping her in the house. David defended himself half-heartedly, mentioning occasions on which he had helped Mrs. B and implying that he never received any recognition. The exchange led to withdrawal and sulking on David's part. I challenged Mrs. B's tremendous anger and wondered whether some of it was not actually meant for her husband. Mrs. B was able to return to the difficulties between her and her husband, saying quite frankly that she had been so angry she could have bashed her husband's head in. When, later in the interview, I repeated these words to her, David came to life again; guffawed, holding his hand over his mouth; and at the same time exchanged glances with Joseph, who was also grinning.

In the face of some discouragement on the part of Mrs. B, who struggled hard to change but did not always succeed, I thought we should take stock and asked each person to express his idea of how matters stood. Mrs. B said for herself that she thought she badgered David less, was less often angry with her sister for small things that annoyed her, and was forcing arguments to come out into the open rather than holding a grudge or letting other people in the family do so. Joseph responded very briefly, saying only that he thought both David and his mother were somewhat better, meaning that they were not fighting so much. Mr. B spoke of his being more understanding of David and of his desiring to be even more so. David, who had previously recognized that his mother had been more patient with him, had withdrawn in response to his mother's attack and was not willing to say anything positive.

Even though the B's did not ask me, I volunteered to give my own opinion. (Mrs. B said she was almost afraid to ask me but was glad I had volunteered.) I said I thought that the B's, as a family, were on the right track; that they all were working hard; and that since change was difficult for everyone, they should not be discouraged, because I knew from my own experience that change, rather than proceeding directly, ebbed and flowed.

At the end of the session, David asked whether he could take home the tape of the interview. He did not do so directly but used his mother to voice the question. I wondered whether it might not be more advisable to play the tape or part of the tape in the office and said I should like to think about David's question until the next session.

This interview demonstrated clearly that the B family is showing movement but also that the homeostatic mechanisms are strong. Trouble was described, at least during part of the interview, as being between the couple, rather than caused by David. Then, the old scapegoating pattern was in some degree re-established, and David supported it by maintaining unreasonable demands and by turning down offers of attention or gifts when they were made. I hope I can get David to accept individual interviews because the boy needs additional help for himself; anything that may seem to him to constitute pressure must be carefully avoided.

Twelfth Family Interview, December 16

There was a more tolerant atmosphere in the interview. There was much smiling, particularly between David and his mother, which underscored the special alliance, negative and positive, that exists between them. David was much freer with his father, at one time touching his father's shoe with his own in a playful way. There was a great deal of laughter during the session, both during the discussion and when the preceding week's tape was being played.

126

Mrs. B first reported a great improvement in her relationship with her sister, who, again, did not attend the session because she was very tired and sleepy. Mrs. B judged that the easier relationship between her and Miss F had come about because she had been less critical and her sister had responded positively and helped her more with the housework. Then, laughing and pointing to David, Mrs. B said: "This big oaf has cleaned my downstairs, and he has done it so well I myself could not have done it better." She said she had almost started to cry when she had discovered what David had done—and that David himself had been happy. I expressed my sympathy with her feelings and also my concern about what would happen if David made no similar efforts the following week. Mrs. B laughed and said that David had already informed her his cleaning job was "for the year." She added that she did not expect David to do such a job often but was very pleased he had been proving himself to be so capable. She now knew, she said, that he could do all kinds of things and could take care of himself.

Mrs. B then told me that David had expressed uncertainty to her about what I meant by saying that he must figure out what he wanted for himself. As we discussed the topic, I heard for the first time from Mrs. B that David had mentioned he would like to go into cancer research. This fact gave me an opportunity to raise with David the issue of his having gotten behind in his schoolwork and to point out how it might hamper him. I suggested that perhaps his principal difficulty was an inability to concentrate on anything for any length of time, even if he wanted to. David at first did not say anything, but after I insisted that it was important for me to know whether or not I was right, he very clearly said that I was. I then suggested that David make his own appointment with me, and though there was much discussion about the day and hour, there was really no basic resistance on David's part and an appointment separate from the family session was made.

I admired David's new jacket and was told that he had selected it himself. Mrs. B then turned to the topic of smoking and her pride in David for having stopped smoking for a time, even though he had since told her that he could not continue his abstinence. The topic was discussed for a while; I praised David for his will power and stressed that it was very difficult not to smoke when other people in the environment did—as did Mr. B, who had tried several times to stop but always resumed the habit. There was some talk about the children's wishing for a pool table and also some talk about the possibility of the family's going to the country, at least for a day, since the B's could not afford a week-end trip. Mr. B spoke positively about breakfasttime the previous Sunday, when David had come downstairs at ten o'clock and the entire family had had breakfast together, pleasantly rather than unpleasantly.

Then David's wish to hear the tape of the previous interview was supported by the other family members, and the tape was put on. The B's all listened intently. When Joseph said something at one time while the tape was playing, David immediately said, "Sh." As soon as Mrs. B heard her voice getting angry, she remarked, "I sound like a real shrew." David, with a grin, covered his face when his mother imitated his grumbling voice as it came from the tape. When Mr. B's voice was coming from the tape complaining about his disappointment at his wife's not being at breakfast, Mrs. B said, "He sounds really pathetic," and then added that it seemed to her he was jealous of her attention to the children. Mrs. B remarked that the tape was wonderful in that it could show them what they had been like. When, also on the tape, Mr. B said that he would see to it that the following Sunday's breakfast would be pleasant, Joseph jokingly remarked that breakfast would indeed be pleasant because his father would save all the arguments for dinner. Everybody laughed. Mrs. B remarked that Joseph had not gotten a word in during the taping. While some pointed questions of mine were heard, I said, "I seem to be saying pretty mean things sometimes," but there was no time for the family to respond. At one time Mrs. B remarked, pointing to me, "She always sides with David," but she said it laughingly, exchanging glances with David that were almost flirtatious. When Joseph laughed at one time at Mrs. B's anger, she said good-naturedly to him, "Oh, keep quiet." At one point in the tape at which Mrs. B was talking calmly, after her angry outburst, she said, "I sound so nice here!"

Both Mr. and Mrs. B spoke about the value of hearing the tape, and Mrs. B said she thought many families should have such an opportunity to listen to themselves. When I said that family interviews shortened the time span of help needed by families, Mrs. B added, "Yes, and it is also much more effective." David was eager to take another tape home, and I acceded to his request. I wished the B's a nice week end—and a nice Sunday breakfast. Mr. B, with a smile, answered, "Yes, we will definitely have a nice breakfast."

During the interview I had warned the family members that Mrs. B or anybody else might get angry again within the next several days and that they should not be distressed by such an occurrence, because it was merely human. Over-all, the atmosphere of the session was one of unprecedented relaxed togetherness. Moreover, Mrs. B achieved an important insight: "Tell me," she said, "whether I am right or wrong. When I heard myself and my husband on that tape, it looked like we did not give David a chance to get in and say something at all." I agreed with her observation and pointed out that it is not easy to absorb such thoughts. There were times when the B's smiles disappeared and their faces became serious—and there was no doubt that David, as well as the others, was aware of his grumbling and the defensive way in which he sometimes answered.

David needs individual help, and there is basis for hope that he is ready to take it at this time.

First Individual Interview with David, December 23

David came into the office badly bitten and scratched by a neighborhood cat he had picked up. He was even quieter than usual and reported that he had been at the hospital, had "shots," and fainted. He knew the family interview had been cancelled because both parents had colds. He himself would have liked to postpone his interview but had kept his appointment because he did not want his mother to get mad at him. David's newest vocational dream is to become a veterinarian.

It was not easy to induce David to talk; however, he did voice some willingness to be retested and to have some remedial help. He was worried about the expense and otherwise understandably ambivalent. While I made it clear that I was not "neutral," but thought David needed help, I suggested he think the matter over. When I gave him a choice between my seeing him alone once more and our talking the matter over in the next family interview, he chose the latter.

Individual interviews with David resulted in his referral to a psychologist trained in remedial teaching.

Follow-up Family Interview, October 19

When I telephoned Mrs. B to make an appointment for a follow-up interview, she said our thoughts must have met because she had just decided she wanted to call me.

The interview was true to form inasmuch as again it was started negatively. David had been attacked in the street, without reason, by two boys and had ended up with a black eye. When Mrs. B told me about the incident, David was furious, saying that he did not like his mother's telling the story to everyone; he did not give any specific reason for his anger but insisted that the story was "nobody's business." Subsequently Mrs. B complained about David's having resumed his association with a friend whom she has always thought to have a bad influence on him. Nevertheless, after a while, Mrs. B said that she had really wanted to start the session positively by telling me that David had been "a wonderful boy" all summer, all she had always wanted him to be. He had worked at the hospital; come home at night at the prescribed time, been more amicable with Joseph; and kept up with his remedial reading. Mrs. B also said, however, that David was often very ungiving, many times rejecting her expressions of interest in him.

Mrs. B then spoke of a particular negative incident of the recent past: David and some friends had taken some glasses from a restaurant and brought them home. David retorted by attacking his father, insisting that his father, too, was dishonest in such little matters. Mr. B at first violently denied the accusation but then admitted he had done such things when he was "a little boy." I said that David, having lived within the family for so many years, must have taken in some of his parents' values. I suggested it was too late for Mrs. B to start to establish other values for David and that he should make his own decisions about right and wrong and live up to them. David looked at me without saying anything, but upon questioning, voiced agreement. He wants to be on his own.

David was working in the hospital with animals, which had always been his first love. Mr. B reported that, even though he had forbidden David to bring animals home from the hospital, since the family had a dog and cat, David had nevertheless brought home a guinea pig; then, when Mr. B had set a time limit for the animal's return to the hospital, David had not adhered to it. Mr. B argued that David and Joseph did not take proper care of the animals they already had and that the burden of their failure to do so fell on him. I asked why Mr. B did not let the boys see the animals' unhappiness if they forgot to feed them or give them water, and Mr. B said he simply did not have the heart to leave the animals uncared for. I sided with Mr. B when he said there were certain things he could decide in his own house and suggested that David would have to learn to give and take. Joseph is doing better work in school. When I asked him how he liked the accelerated class, David challenged that word *accelerated,* and some of his old jealousy of Joseph seemed to flare up. Even so, both boys said they were getting along better.

When I finally asked about the marital relationship, I learned that Mr. B's slightly increased self-assertion had not lasted long, and though he did not speak directly of the sexual relationship, he made me understand that he had not gone to see a doctor as he had intended. Mr. B's earnings have recently increased, and he feels relieved after a bad summer. Mrs. B still feels it to be an imposition that she has to be the financial mainstay of the family because of the irregularity of Mr. B's income and the substantial indebtedness of the family, recently increased because of David's need for tutoring. There had been no money for recreation, but the family had gone bowling several times at a free bowling alley. There was at least no bitterness between the couple; Mrs. B was somewhat resigned and Mr. B continued to hope that he could prove himself financially.

In summarizing the changes that family counseling has brought about for the B family, it can be said that there is a definite change for the better. David is no longer the scapegoat; he receives much positive attention from both his parents, as well as some negative attention. He has continued his tutorial lessons, which may help him to graduate normally from high school. He will still have a difficult adolescence because of his impaired ability to communicate, particularly positive feelings, and because of a considerable amount of accumulated hostility. Nevertheless, he expresses hostility more directly than he did formerly and no longer transfers it from his parents to Joseph. The marital relationship has become more bearable to Mrs. B because she has been able to ventilate with the counselor her true feelings about her husband, including her frequent inclination to leave him. For a while, at least, Mrs. B has been able to lean on the counselor and thus has had some of her dependency needs fulfilled. Mr. B, who is somewhat limited intellectually, has somehow understood that he must work to develop a do-as-I-do rather than do-as-I-say attitude toward his sons. If this family could overcome its financial insecurity and if Mrs. B could work less and the family could have some fun together, all family members would benefit greatly. However, the achievement of such a status is doubtful.

Mrs. B seemed the one who was not quite ready for ending. I invited her to call me whenever she felt she needed me, and she said she had wanted me to encourage her to do so. I added that since the other family members did not want further service, future interviews could be for her alone.

The B's thanked me for my help, and the interview was ended on a humorous note when I imitated David's gruff voice, saying, "Goodbye, David, and don't say a word too many." He grinned. So, too, did Joseph when I said I knew he had been very bored and would have much preferred a ball game or a circus to our family discussions. The leave-taking had much warmth in it.

130

ANALYSIS OF RELATIONSHIPS IN THE B FAMILY

Some Parental Goals

1. Education for children (general and religious) beyond parents' level
2. Some recognition outside family (job of Mrs. B; volunteer work of Mr. B at synagogue)
3. Financial security (effort to get rid of debts)
4. Good name in neighborhood (distress at David's "bad name")
5. A well-kept home

The Carrying of Roles

Mr. B's Roles

1. Breadwinner
2. Father
3. Volunteer worker
4. Husband
   For Mrs. B, not fulfilling expectations as 1 and 2 (mainly 1) and partially fulfilling role as 4. For David, not fulfilling expectations as 2. For himself, fulfilling expectations as 3.

Mrs. B's Roles

1. Breadwinner
2. Mother
3. Wife
   For Mr. B, fulfilling expectations as 1, 2, 3. For David, not satisfactorily fulfilling role as 2. For herself, fulfilling role as 1, but also resenting it.

David's Roles

1. Son of father
2. Son of mother
3. Brother of Joseph
4. Student
   In general, not fulfilling expectations as 1, 2, 3, and 4.

Joseph's Roles

1. Son of father
2. Son of mother
3. Brother of David
4. Student
   For Mr. and Mrs. B, fulfilling expectations as 1, 2, and 3. For David, not fulfilling expectations as 3. In general, not fulfilling expectations as 4.

Family Relationship Pattern

Mr. B to Mrs. B

Mr. B leans on Mrs. B: he admires her and looks to her to fulfill his great dependency needs. He evades telling of distressing matters and covers up his feelings of anger and resentment. He responds passively and indirectly.

Mr. B to David

Mr. B sees David as the source of all family disturbance and makes him the scapegoat. Mr. B puts on David some of his responsibility as the man in the house and resents David's refusal to carry this role.

Mr. B to Joseph

Mr. B is protective of Joseph, the only family member who is completely nonthreatening to him. He and Joseph are the "weak" part of the family.

Mrs. B to Mr. B

Mrs. B wants to protect Mr. B and also enjoys her feelings of superiority (his admiration) and her anger. But she also resents not being able to lean on him and having to take on so much responsibility.

Mrs. B to David

Mrs. B sees David as a source of disturbance and discomfort and makes him the scapegoat. She resents his not conforming to her standards and his failure to give her the opportunity to be proud of him.

Mrs. B. to Joseph

Mrs. B protects "the little one," feeling warmly toward him because he gratifies her by conforming in large measure to her standards.

David to Mrs. B

Being very dependent on Mrs. B and resenting her demands and critical attitude, David is very hostile toward his mother. He responds to her angry outbursts with withdrawal and acting out.

David to Mr. B

David has some positive feeling toward Mr. B but only very limited respect for him; he realizes he is expected to do as Mr. B *says,* not as he *does.* David imitates Mr. B's passive-aggressive pattern. He is angry about Mr. B's demands and critical attitude.

David to Joseph

David is ambivalent toward Joseph, needing him as a companion and, at the same time, being jealous of him as the "favorite". He uses Joseph to retaliate against Mrs. B, through hurting him verbally and physically.

Joseph to Mr. and Mrs. B

Joseph "gets along" by compliance. He has begun to fall down in his schoolwork as "passive resistance" to parental demands. Moreover, unconsciously, he dares not surpass David.

Joseph to David

Joseph yields to David; he needs him. He has some fear of David's violence.

Shift in Family Relationships During the Treatment Period

Mrs. B begins to let go of her role as the one in the family responsible for everyone else, pushing everyone toward *her* goal. She tries to accept reality, particularly Mr. B's limitations.

Mr. B becomes somewhat more active and more direct in expressing anger toward Mrs. B. He becomes somewhat more tolerant of David.

David is expressing anger directly. He begins to work out his hostility toward Mrs. B, though he remains hostile, in some measure, both toward his parents and toward Joseph. He is developing some positive feelings, chiefly toward Mr. B. He is no longer acting out and is taking on some responsibility for improving his school performance, because *he* wants to.

Joseph, who had taken on his father's and brother's pattern of passivity, is becoming more responsible in doing schoolwork. He is less afraid of David's "bullying."

In the discussion of the Brownstein case emphasis was placed on the first interview, although the balance of the case record, read by the staff before the session, enhanced understanding of the counseling process. An analysis of the discussion follows.

Objectives of the beginning family group interviews and early diagnostic considerations were identified:

1. To gain a general understanding of family relationships and family strengths and weaknesses and to find a tentative answer to the question why David, the primary client, had such low self-esteem that he stole and lied.

In the psychiatric conference, the consultant tentatively diagnosed David as having a character disorder, passive-aggressive type, verging on schizophrenia. Use of family group counseling as a means of understanding David's position and role in the family was considered preferable to referral of David for psychiatric treatment.

2. To determine which family member was the central figure in decision-making, it being recognized that, in some cases, there may be a shift as family counseling continues and that the balance of forces may change.

Mrs. B was clearly the governing figure in the first interview and retained that role throughout the entire treatment period.

3. To determine how the health-pathology balance of each family member affected family interrelationships, taking into consideration the needs of each individual in the family constellation.

Mr. B had lost his mother early in his life and sought, in some measure, to find a mother-substitute in Mrs. B. Mrs. B had feminine dependency needs that neither she nor her husband recognized because she appeared to be strong. Failing in his masculine role as husband and father, Mr. B frus-

133

trated her. He was sexually impotent, inadequate as a breadwinner, and lacking in interest in his home and children. He sought satisfaction from his community work rather than from his family. Mrs. B gained satisfaction from having others dependent on her. She was confused in her role as a mother, because she had idealized her own mother, who had been demanding rather than giving. Unsatisfied by her husband, Mrs. B became demanding of David. David identified with his father, resented his mother's demands, and imitated his father's passive-aggressive pattern. Mrs. B rejected both her husband and David as failures, and her rejection together with her lack of respect for her husband interfered with David's psychosexual development and his masculine self-image. David had begun to react by acting out, but when his behavior did not protect him from anxiety, he began to withdraw from relationships.

David and Joseph were inclined to fight each other, but in the family interview a positive tie between them could be observed. Since Mrs. B projected her frustrations with Mr. B onto David, it was not necessary for her to use Joseph as a scapegoat. Joseph's failure in school appeared to be, at least in part, the result of an unconscious fear of being punished by David if he succeeded where David had failed. In the first interview, Joseph was protected by both parents.

4. To set realistic, clear goals for counseling, derived from the dynamics of the immediate session but taking into account the strengths and weaknesses of all family members.

At first it appeared that Mrs. B was the primary problem in the family, since she ruled the roost and estranged the other members by her nagging and general discontent, but Mr. B's inordinate dependency needs and his inability to feel and behave as a father to his boys became obvious in the process of family group interviewing. In spite of his limited ego strength, Mr. B had to be encouraged to take more responsibility in the family, for the benefit of the family as a whole and also for the purpose of bringing about much-needed improvement in his self-image. It was thought that the family homeostasis could shift only to a limited extent. When Mrs. B revealed her wish for support, it became clear that Mr. B was threatened by the signs of change in a life-long pattern. Mrs. B could be helped to fill her role as a wife and to exercise her authority as a mother in a somewhat gentler, less critical manner. An important goal for David was to free him from his mother's control in such measure that he could assert himself at least in finding his own goals, including remedial help. It was important to let him know that he had not had a chance as a young child to resist his mother's demands but that he was now strong enough to do so without fear of being destroyed.

Some approaches to treatment were identified:

1. Removing the onus of blame and guilt from the identified client—the one whose symptoms prompt the family to seek help—and shifting attention to the treatment of a family problem.

2. Helping family members recognize and communicate their feelings about each other and expectations of each other.

134

3. Helping family members recognize alliances and double messages; helping them communicate clearly.

4. Seeking to remove blocks to improvement through individual or dyadic interviews when appropriate.

5. Seeking to develop relationships with all family members, while avoiding alliances, and helping all members become involved in counseling.

6. Helping family members get a true picture of their relationships and their individual behavior (playing back tapes can be effective).

7. Emphasizing the positive quality in family relationships and the health in individual family members; giving hope, on a realistic basis, that the family's situation can improve.

8. Creating an informal atmosphere to cut through tensions (humor can be effective).

A difference of opinion emerged during the discussion about whether or not the parents' sexual problems should have been discussed in the presence of the children. There was agreement, however, about the factors to be taken into consideration in reaching a decision: the ages of the children, the nature of the sexual problem, the extent of the children's knowledge of it, and the ability of the parents to speak about it in the children's presence.

There was also a brief discussion of the specific differences in the counselor's role when conducting a family session as against an individual interview. It was agreed that in a family session the counselor's main task is to facilitate interchange and direct communication between the family members and that, at the same time, he must be prepared to become, temporarily, an important part of the family.